D1511000

Learning-Based
Client-Centered
Therapy

Learning-Based Client-Centered Therapy

David G. Martin
University of Manitoba

Brooks/Cole Publishing Company
Monterey, California

A Division of Wadsworth Publishing Company, Inc.
Belmont, California

RC 481
M34

This book was edited by Konrad Kerst and designed by Linda Marcetti. It was typeset by Datagraphics, Inc., Phoenix, Arizona, and printed and bound by Malloy Lithographing, Inc., Ann Arbor, Michigan.

© 1972 by Wadsworth Publishing Company, Inc., Belmont, California 94002. All rights reserved. No part of this book may be reproduced, stored in a retrieval system, or transcribed, in any form or by any means—electronic, mechanical, photocopying, recording, or otherwise—without the prior written permission of the publisher: Brooks/Cole Publishing Company, Monterey, California, a division of Wadsworth Publishing Company, Inc.

ISBN: 0-8185-0022-0
L.C. Catalog Card No: 73-178812
Printed in the United States of America

1 2 3 4 5 6 7 8 9 10————77 76 75 74 73 72

To my parents,
for teaching me
and freeing me to see things
in new combinations

Preface

The field of psychotherapy seems to be moving away from adamant commitment to schools of therapy and toward a rapprochement among many positions—particularly between learning and client-centered approaches. In this book I maintain and hopefully demonstrate that a sufficiently complex learning view of neurosis provides a basis for explaining the efficacy of empathy-oriented therapy and for specifying the circumstances in which behavior-modification techniques are most appropriate.

Each therapist is a blend of the effects of his training, the influences of his colleagues, and his experience. In a sense, this book presents my particular blend at this stage in my career. I have found this blend effective in my own practice and teaching, and I am presenting it in the hope that it will be useful to both practicing therapists and therapists in training. As I wrote the book, I felt myself talking to graduate students and to my professional colleagues. My orientation is empathy-based therapy, but the influence I would most like to have is on the learning approach to behavior change; one of my major themes is that we need to avoid oversimplistic analysis and application of learning principles.

At one time this book was the second half of a longer manuscript. The first half was written to the undergraduate and has since been published as a separate book, *Introduction to Psychotherapy* (Martin, 1971). *Learning-Based Client-Centered Therapy*, although much more advanced, includes theoretical material that is also covered in the first book; I felt that some repetition of material was necessary to clarify the application of my theoretical thinking to the practice of therapy.

The manuscript was greatly strengthened by helpful reviews from Erasmus Hoch and Edward L. Walker, both of the University of Michigan; I have also incorporated some of the suggestions offered by Frank Auld of the University of Windsor and Kingsley Ferguson of the Clarke Institute of Psychiatry, Toronto, both of whom were discussants at a workshop based on this book. Typing was done with care and promptness by Anne Greaves, Pam Gingera, and Dorothy Savage.

As always, I owe the most to the people I live with—to my wife, Nona, and our children, Joel, Laura, and Kathy. They make it all worth the effort.

David G. Martin

Contents

Learning-Based Client-Centered Therapy

1

Posing the problem

The practicing psychotherapist and the student in training both face a bewildering diversity of schools of treatment. The existence of schools of psychotherapy has both helped and hurt the advancement of knowledge about the treatment of emotional disorder. Adamant, semi-religious commitment to one position may even be a necessary part of treatment when knowledge is scarce and therapy depends heavily on the client's hope. However, personal investment in a theory seems also to have rigidified many therapists and made it difficult for them to hear what other approaches might offer. Others' ideas are often dismissed with scorn —usually because of an inaccurate view of the other approach. In a field as young as psychotherapy it seems unlikely that any one approach is a complete answer. We need to keep rebuilding our systems, drawing from established therapies, restating ideas that may seem dissimilar only because they have been said in different words, and synthesizing approaches in the light of new knowledge. The practicing therapist must be open to change—and even

1

seek it—while having enough confidence in his current position to honestly offer services he believes will help his client. He must be a loyal revisionist believer, holding firmly to his tentative position.

Challenges to psychotherapy

Synthesis becomes easier and adamant commitment less necessary as our research advances. We are still stumbling, but we seem to be stumbling forward. At least two serious challenges to the field of psychotherapy have made it clear that research is absolutely imperative. Without it psychotherapy will not only stagnate but will face rejection by other professionals and ultimately by the public.

The first of these challenges was instituted primarily by Eysenck (1952, 1954, 1955a, 1955b, 1961, 1964). He states: "Roughly two-thirds of a group of neurotic patients will recover or improve to a marked extent within about two years of the onset of their illness, whether they are treated by means of psychotherapy or not" (1952, p. 322). There is no evidence, Eysenck argues, that psychotherapy is more effective than no treatment at all. The Great Outcome Debate was quickly joined and continues to rage. Eysenck's conclusions were attacked by many (Rosenzweig, 1954; Cartwright, 1955; deCharmes, Levy, & Wertheimer, 1954; Stevenson, 1959; Strupp, 1963). Kiesler (1966) has summarized the arguments against Eysenck's position as being that the patient groups Eysenck used for his comparison were in many vital ways not comparable groups; that the no-treatment neurotic groups Eysenck used actually had received a form of psychotherapy; that the criteria for improvement or recovery were grossly different in the samples Eysenck was comparing; and that, in fact, other surveys of untreated neurotics had much lower recovery rates than the two-thirds figure reported by Eysenck (Hastings, 1958; Saslow & Peters, 1956). In his original article, and again more recently, Eysenck (1964) has readily acknowledged some of the shortcomings of his comparisons and has said that "the figures quoted do not necessarily disprove the possibility of therapeutic usefulness." Eysenck has taken the position that he may not have demonstrated that psychotherapy is not effective, but neither has anyone else demonstrated that it *is* effective. In order to maintain this position and support his firm commitment to behavior therapy,

Eysenck has had to ignore or dismiss evidence on the efficacy of client-centered therapy. In forcing the field of psychotherapy in the direction of research, however, Eysenck has performed a valuable service. Public relations and the hard sell are inappropriate bases for the survival of psychotherapy.

A second challenge to the field of psychotherapy was Bergin's observation (1963, 1966) of "the deterioration effect." From his analysis and reinterpretation of a number of published research studies, Bergin made the observation that "Psychotherapy may cause people to become better or worse adjusted than comparable people who do not receive such treatment" (1966, p. 240). It looked as though some therapists were indeed consistently causing improvement in their clients, but at the same time others were actually causing deterioration. Ironically, this disturbing observation is both a serious challenge to psychotherapy and a partial answer to Eysenck's criticism, since if some therapists are causing growth and some are causing deterioration, psychotherapy would, on the average, appear to be ineffective. If some psychotherapists *are* doing damage (as seems to be the case), it is absolutely incumbent upon those in the field to identify the therapist characteristics and behaviors that are responsible both for improvement and for deterioration. Bergin noted that some progress in this direction has been made within the last few years. For example, some studies related successful therapy to high levels of Rogers' therapeutic conditions—nonpossessive warmth, accurate empathy, and, to some extent, congruence. Many of these studies also provide some confirmation of the deterioration effect, in that those clients who received high levels of Rogers' therapeutic conditions showed improvement at high rates, while those who received low levels either deteriorated relative to control clients or had unexpectedly low improvement rates. Bergin also noted the emerging evidence for the efficacy of behavior-modification techniques and drew other implications of research for practice in therapy.[1]

In a sense, this book is an attempt to respond to Bergin's challenge by specifying the elements of therapy that make it effective and

[1]Bergin's observation of the deterioration effect has been challenged by Braucht (1970), but Bergin (1970) has rebutted Braucht's arguments and concluded: "In general, the case for the deterioration effect is much greater today than it was when the original article was published" (p. 302).

those that cause deterioration. I am making an attempt at systematic, internally consistent eclectic synthesis—given what we know now. It will have to be rewritten in a few years as new knowledge appears and as I learn things I should already know. But for now, current research, theory, and personal experience will be the bases for developing a theoretical model and applying the model to the practice of therapy.

Development of a model for psychotherapy

A brief personal note will help clarify how the ideas in the following chapters were developed. I received my early training in psychotherapy at the University of Chicago Counseling Center, which was founded by Carl Rogers. As a result of my experiences and relationships with other staff members there, I developed a strong commitment to client-centered and humanistic thinking. Near the end of my career as a graduate student, I spent an internship year in Chicago at the Institute for Juvenile Research, which at that time had a primarily psychoanalytic orientation. My internship year left me, if anything, more firmly committed to client-centered thinking, as a result of my experience and reading of the research literature. My first job, however, was in the psychology department and the Counseling Service of the University of Iowa, one of the most firmly learning-theory-oriented psychology departments in existence. It was through the process of long and sometimes painful theoretical arguments that it became clear to me that a number of the basic theoretical underpinnings of client-centered thinking were difficult to defend in the light of evidence collected in the field of psychology. This was especially true of the view of man as innately self-actualizing, a view essential to Rogers' theory.

I was faced with a dilemma. It was difficult to defend some key theoretical notions in client-centered thinking, but my experience and what was by then a considerable portion of the research available seemed to indicate that client-centered therapy was effective. In fact, the evidence led Bergin to state that "to date the only school of interview-oriented psychotherapy which has consistently yielded positive outcomes in research studies is the client-centered approach" (1966, p. 238); since 1966, evidence has appeared to support the efficacy of behavior modification, a possibility that Bergin anticipated in his article. In addition to the evidence Bergin cited to support his statement about client-centered therapy (Rogers & Dymond, 1954; Shlien, Mosak, & Dreikurs, 1962; Truax & Carkhuff, 1963), much other evidence has indicated either that therapists describing themselves as client-centered demonstrated effective results or that the measurement of the central attributes of client-centered therapy (accurate empathy, warmth, and genuineness) could be related to successful outcome in psychotherapy (Truax & Carkhuff, 1967; Van Der Veen, 1967; Bierman, 1969). In the process of several years of arguments and discussions with students and colleagues, I began to resolve my dilemma by developing a theoretical model of psychotherapy, within the general limits of learning theory, which could account for the therapeutic effectiveness of accurate empathy, warmth, and genuineness.

It is an interesting sidelight that the development of a theoretical model helped me discover some of my own misunderstanding of the nature of empathy and forced me to modify some of my practices as a therapist. As the model developed I also began to see similarities among various schools of psychotherapy, and it became possible to understand that many therapists seem to be doing similar things but describing their actions in different words.[2] More recently, an expanding literature and the sometimes gentle prodding of respected colleagues led to my incorporating behavior-modification techniques in the general model. I hope my theoretical model will serve as a vehicle for integrating some of the diversity that now exists and for helping practicing therapists and therapists in training to translate their theoretical thinking into practice and their experience into useful theoretical thinking.

In more formal terms, the model should serve at least four major purposes: (1) *Forming testable concepts.* One practice that has led to misunderstanding and disagreement in the psychotherapy literature has been the imprecise use of words and the failure to define words adequately, especially when describing behavior. To be

[2]In his classic study, Fiedler (1950) presented evidence that experienced therapists were very similar in their behavior regardless of their theoretical orientation. Later evidence (Strupp, 1955a, 1955b, 1957) indicated that Fiedler's analysis may have been oversimplified, but many writers have commented on the similarities and congruences among the different schools of psychotherapy (Patterson, 1966).

most useful, a theory must use explicitly defined words, and it must describe behavior in a way that permits others to observe it. (2) *Incorporating previous knowledge.* A major function of theory is to clarify the future; a theory is useless, however, if it does not incorporate all relevant present knowledge in an internally consistent way. (3) *Generating predictions.* A theory forces the organization of present knowledge in such a way that relationships that were not seen before become apparent. These relationships then provide the basis for making predictions about behavior that can be verified through research. (4) *Guiding future practice.* The functions of a theoretical model for therapy are obviously not all scientific; we are also interested in improving the practice of psychotherapy. If a theoretical model helps to organize our knowledge and to make differential predictions about different kinds of therapist behavior, it provides the basis for modifying the practice of psychotherapy and for modifying the way people are taught to be psychotherapists.

Limits of the model. Kiesler (1966) has pointed out that one of the myths of psychotherapy is the "uniformity assumption." By this Kiesler means that psychotherapy is often conceived of as only one kind of treatment—one that is appropriate for all emotional disorders. Since different kinds of emotional disorders have different causes, different kinds of treatments are probably necessary for their relief. With this thought in mind, I am offering the analysis presented in this book only as appropriate treatment for anxiety-based neuroses. These disorders are discussed more thoroughly in Chapter 3. You will see that some of these disorders are best treated in empathy-oriented therapy, while others seem more suitable for behavior-modification techniques.

There are three major emotional disorders that might better be treated by techniques other than ones designed to reduce anxiety. First, psychologists are sometimes called on to deal with reactions to extreme situational stress affecting the behavior of otherwise emotionally healthy individuals. Rather than techniques oriented to changing the individual, the most appropriate treatment in some such cases is manipulation of the environment to relieve the situational stress. Second, psychopathic or acting-out behavior may well be an anxiety-reducing symptom, like other neurotic symptoms (see the treatment of this issue in Chapter 3). In other cases, however, what is called psychopathy may be the result of a lack of appropriate socialization training ("too little anxiety") or even an inordinate need for stimulation. In the first case, a treatment designed to reduce anxiety might be appropriate, whereas in other cases the same treatment might worsen the condition. Third, I have excluded schizophrenia and the other psychoses from this analysis of therapy—more out of ignorance of the etiology of schizophrenia than for any other reason. The psychological treatment of the psychoses has posed a difficult and frustrating question for all schools of psychotherapy. It seems quite likely that genetic and/or physiological factors complicate the etiology of the psychoses, and psychotic patients are often not amenable to interview-oriented treatment conditions. Rogers, Gendlin, Kiesler, & Truax (1967) have recently reported a long-term study of client-centered therapy with schizophrenics and have reported mixed results. Overall improvement rates of therapy patients were quite disappointing, but some analyses indicated that patients receiving high therapeutic conditions (accurate empathy, warmth, and genuineness) demonstrated greater improvement than those who received low therapeutic conditions. In a nine-year follow-up of schizophrenic patients, Truax (1970) reported that patients who had received high levels of empathy, regard, and congruence tended to spend fewer days in the hospital over the nine years than patients who had received no therapy; patients who had received therapy characterized by low levels of the therapeutic conditions tended to spend more days in the hospital than untreated patients. These findings suggest the possibility that client-centered therapy might be appropriate for schizophrenic disorders, but since the present theoretical development deals only with the etiology of neurosis, the treatment of schizophrenia will be considered an open question. Also, since the treatment discussed in this book may be inappropriate for some cases and may even do damage, it seems incumbent upon those practicing psychotherapy to make some diagnostic decisions, at least within the broad framework of whether the problem being treated is the result of an anxiety-based neurosis or is caused by different factors.

Theoretical foundations of the model. The view of man's nature on which this theoretical model is based is, in general, the view proposed by learning theorists, with one major modification. Understanding the model for therapy requires the understanding and acceptance of only the broad outlines of learning theory: the ubiquitous nature of reinforcement, classical and instrumental conditioning, primary and secondary sources of drive, and the nature of frustration and conflict.

A modification of learning theory proposed by Butler and Rice (1963) is the conception of exploratory behavior as innately motivated rather than as only a learned source of motivation (see Chapter 2). The evidence for stimulus hunger as an innate drive in man seems to be strong but is still open to question. If man is indeed innately motivated to seek new experiences, my analysis of therapy will be enhanced. The present theoretical model, however, could fit solely within more traditional learning theory and is not dependent on the notion of stimulus hunger.

Organization of the book

To establish the need for a systematically eclectic theoretical model, the next chapter presents critical evaluations of the major schools of psychotherapy and a summary statement of the present and probable future status of these approaches. Since these evaluations cannot be extensive, they function more as a personal statement of position than as complete criticisms. They set the stage for the model. A contemporary learning view of the nature of neurosis then leads into a theoretical chapter on conflict relief. The rest of the book is practice-oriented: the theoretical framework is fleshed out with suggested techniques useful to a systematically eclectic therapist.

2

Critical evaluations

The critical evaluations in this chapter assume considerable familiarity with the major schools of therapy: psychoanalytic, client-centered (as a representative of humanistic therapies), and learning-oriented approaches.[1]

To repeat, these evaluations are not exhaustive analyses. They more nearly are a position statement designed to establish the need for a theoretical model within the limits set in the last chapter. Some will object that important positions have been omitted, which is true. In another book (Martin, 1971) I have evaluated a number of other approaches, but even there, limitations of space and of purpose forced the omission of many of the dozens of theories alive today. The approaches included here are those that seem to represent the major influences on both the field in general

[1]More complete summaries of these approaches, along with critical evaluations, can be found in *Introduction to Psychotherapy* (Martin, 1971), an appropriate source for readers not familiar with all the approaches discussed.

and on the development of the model to be presented. At the end of this chapter a summary briefly states the position from which I developed the model.

Psychoanalysis

Psychoanalysis was once by far the most potent force in the field of psychotherapy. Its influence has clearly waned in recent years, partly because its theoretical underpinnings have been questioned or rejected, and partly because of the lack of research supporting the position (Strupp & Bergin, 1969). It is fair to say, however, that almost every practicing psychotherapist owes a debt to some of Freud's ideas. Freud's contributions to the understanding of personality include the notion of *unconscious influences* on behavior; the fact that *behavior develops genetically*—that is, is influenced by early experiences; the notion of *psychic causality*—that behavior obeys laws and is caused by antecedent conditions; and an increased understanding of *the role of sexuality* in personality development.

The evaluations and criticisms of psychoanalysis have been voluminous, a fact that attests to the important role it has played in psychology. These evaluations of psychoanalysis can be best summarized under three headings: theory, practice, and research.

Theory. The notion of psychic energy and Freud's construction of the topography of the mind are extremely difficult to defend in the light of modern psychological knowledge. It now seems most reasonable to think of mental functioning as brain functioning, and few psychologists today would argue for the existence of a "mind," much less of an "unconscious mind." Many brain functions *are* unconscious and influence behavior, but these functions are more precisely conceived as unconscious *processes*. Freud himself, in his last book, consistently referred to "unconscious phenomena" rather than to "the unconscious."

One of the greatest difficulties with psychoanalytic theory has been its tendency to be expressed in personalized ways. Its concepts are reified as though they had a separate existence. The writing of Freud (1935) and many of his followers is exemplified by language such as "the ego comes to a decision," "instincts can turn the ego back into a portion of the id," "the ego becomes aware," "The superego battles with the id," and "thoughts are pushed back into the unconscious," which is seen as a different *place* than the conscious, since the mind is seen as "topographical, by which we mean that it has to do with the spatial relationships we assume within the mind." Many psychoanalysts readily acknowledge that they no longer conceive of the ego, for example, as an entity or a thing but refer to ego *processes.* This distinction would be acceptable to most psychologists, but it is then difficult to understand why references continue to be made to *the* ego or to "ego boundaries" and similar constructs. In some cases, the preservation of Freud's terminology seems to have been more important than conceptual clarity of language. The current status of Freud's theories is summarized well by a contemporary analyst (Marmor, 1968) in his editor's introduction to a collection of articles entitled *Modern Psychoanalysis:*

Psychoanalysis traditionally has been considered to be three things: a *method* of investigation of thoughts and feelings of which the subject is unaware ["the unconscious"], a *theory* of human personality, and a *technique* of therapy. At this point in history ... the value of [Freud's] psychoanalytic *method* of investigating "unconscious" mental processes remains unquestioned. ... However, as many of the chapters in this volume amply demonstrate, classical psychoanalysis as a *theory* of human behavior has not equally withstood the test of time; but this statement requires qualification. I do not wish to imply that all of Freud's views have been valueless. Certain of his basic constructs, such as those of conflict, repression, transference, and the "unconscious" still constitute an extremely effective foundation for an understanding of human behavior and psychopathology *despite the fact that the data upon which they were based can be dealt with just as effectively within other frames of reference, such as those of communication theory or learning theory.* What has become obsolete has been the cumbersome metapsychological superstructure that Freud erected upon these fundamental concepts—notably his theory of instincts, of libido, of the tripartite structure of the psyche, and of psychic energy. This "mythology" of psychoanalysis, as Freud once called his theory of instincts, has been rendered untenable by newer developments and findings in the behavioral sciences [pp. 5–6].[2]

Practice. Many characteristics of psychoanalysis have been adopted as standard practice by psychotherapists of different orientations. For example, most psychotherapy is based on talking, and many therapists, although not calling themselves psy-

---

[2]From Marmor, J. (Ed.) *Modern Psychoanalysis.* New York: Basic Books, 1968. Reprinted by permission.

choanalysts, utilize the techniques of free association and interpretation. Dollard and Miller (1950), for instance, have cast many
of the techniques of psychoanalysis into a learning-theory framework. Classical psychoanalysis, however, typically required an
hour a day, five days a week, and often lasted from two to seven
years. Such a treatment technique has not proved economically
feasible except for a very few, and many challenges have been
leveled, even against the efficacy of such intensive applications of
Freud's ideas.

The most aggressive attacks on psychoanalysis have come from
those associated with the position of behavior modification. Eysenck's attacks on psychotherapy (1952) were primarily attacks on
the efficacy of psychoanalysis. As noted in Chapter 1, Eysenck's
argument is vulnerable to criticism, but it is relevant here to say
that acceptable scientific evidence of the effectiveness of psychoanalysis has failed to emerge. Psychoanalytic training still holds
sway at many training centers and institutes, and many therapists
call themselves analytically oriented, but even Marmor (1968) has
expressed regret that "the high promises once held forth by psychoanalysis as a technique of therapy have failed to materialize."
Enrollments at analytically oriented training centers and institutes
have shown some tendency to remain constant or decline slightly,
and it seems likely that Freud's influence on the practice of psychotherapy will be expressed more and more as only one of several
approaches influencing more eclectic methods of psychotherapy.
In fact, later in this book I note instances from the writings of
several analytically oriented therapists whose descriptions of
therapy have considerable relevance to my view of therapy.

Research. Many writers have commented critically on psychoanalysis as a science of personality. Most psychoanalytic personality theory grew out of observations of the memories of persons
who had sought help for neurotic problems. As an observational
technique, psychoanalysis offers a means for deep exploration of
the individual; but it is very vulnerable to observer bias and influence, it involves a highly select and atypical subject population,
and it has led to ill-defined concepts that are difficult to test by the
scientific method. Some research has supported psychoanalytic
notions, but generally it has indicated that the nature of personality does not fit Freud's analytic model as universally as was once

thought. A summary of Freud's surviving contributions and their relationship to personality can be found in Janis, Mahl, Kagan, and Holt (1969). Our concern here is primarily with the role research has played in psychoanalysis as an approach to psychotherapy.

A few studies have supported psychoanalytic ideas. Speisman (1959), referring to Fenichel's writing (1941), demonstrated that *moderately* deep interpretations (perhaps roughly equivalent to interpreting at the preconscious level) were more likely to be followed by nondefensive patient self-exploration than were deep or shallow interpretations. Adler's approach to psychotherapy was compared with client-centered therapy in a study reported by Shlien, Mosak, and Dreikurs (1962), and both techniques seemed to result in positive changes.

There have been a few attempts to study the process of what occurs in an actual session of psychoanalysis, but many analysts have actively resisted the scientific study of treatment. In 1932 the New York Institute of Psychoanalysis even forbade one of its members to make sound recordings of his analytic hours (Ward, 1964). More recent resistance has not been so blatant, but the fact remains that not much systematic research has been done. One reason often given for this lack of research is the contention that the process of analysis is so complex that examination of minute portions of it would be misleading, particularly since currently available technology is inadequate for the study of psychoanalysis. No doubt there is some truth to this position, since a conceptual scheme for studying tape-recorded hours of analysis would be hard to develop. But it could be done, as is attested by attempts to measure the "depth of interpretation" variable (Harway, Dittmann, Raush, Bordin, & Rigler, 1953) and by Strupp's studies comparing the behavior of therapists from different schools of therapy (1955a, 1960). One survey that did attempt to study the process of analysis was Glover's (1940) questionnaire study of actual practices. He sent questionnaires to 29 practicing analysts and received answers from 24, a reasonably good return. Although asking therapists what they do is not a notably valid way to find out what they actually do, Glover's study did reveal an important finding: it indicated that psychoanalysts were, contrary to Freud's writings, behaving in vastly different ways in practicing the "same" approach to therapy.

Beyond these studies, few attempts have been made to study scientifically the usefulness of psychoanalysis as a treatment technique, especially in the area of outcome studies. The effectiveness of analysis has not been scientifically compared to the effectiveness of other treatments or of no treatment at all. It seems fair to say that, although analysis cannot be rejected as a treatment technique on scientific grounds, neither can it be accepted on scientific grounds. The evidence simply does not exist.

Client-centered therapy

Carl Rogers has clearly had an enormous influence on the training of psychotherapists and counselors in North America and therefore has influenced much of the conduct of psychotherapy since the 1940s. Client-centered therapy has been almost exclusively an American phenomenon, having grown up primarily in the academic setting of American universities. Harper (1959) has argued that one cause of Rogers' widespread success is that his philosophy "fits snugly into the American democratic tradition. The client is treated as an equal who has within him the power to 'cure' himself with no need to lean heavily on the wisdom of an authority or expert" (p. 83).

Practice and research. Harper lists a number of other possible causes for Rogers' success, among which is Rogers' research orientation and the acceptance that this orientation has won in science-oriented American universities. Even Rogers' most vociferous critics have given him the credit (sometimes begrudgingly) of having conducted and inspired others to conduct the most extensive research program ever associated with a school of psychotherapy. It might be argued that he must now share this distinction with behavior-modification therapists, but the extent and quality of research Rogerians have done on actual clients in actual psychotherapy have not yet been surpassed. Rogers has consistently maintained that flexibility and continuous reformulation of theoretical ideas are called for by a scientific approach to the field.

Recently, Rogers' contribution has resulted in extensive research measuring his "therapeutic conditions" and relating these conditions to the outcomes of psychotherapy (Rogers *et al.,* 1967; Truax & Carkhuff, 1967; Bierman, 1969). In spite of the difficulties of doing research on psychotherapy, these studies are establishing a fairly large and reliable body of evidence consistent with Rogers' description of the effective therapeutic process.

Rogers' ideas have consistently aroused controversy and strong reactions—reactions which Rogers says:

continue to surprise me. From my point of view I have felt that I have always put forth my thoughts in a tentative manner, to be accepted or rejected by the reader or the student. But at different times and places psychologists, counselors, and educators have been moved to great wrath, scorn, and criticism by my views. As this furore has tended to die down in these fields it has in recent years been renewed among psychiatrists, some of whom sense, in my way of working, a deep threat to many of their most cherished and unquestioned principles.

Interestingly, Rogers continues this quotation by saying:

And perhaps the storms of criticism are more than matched by the damage done by uncritical and unquestioning "disciples"—individuals who have acquired something of a new point of view for themselves and have gone forth to do battle with all and sundry, using as weapons both inaccurate and accurate understandings of me and my work. I have found it difficult to know, at times, whether I have been hurt more by my "friends" or my enemies [1961, p. 15].[3]

The criticisms of Rogers have fallen roughly within two general areas: (1) the efficacy and breadth of applicability of his therapeutic techniques and (2) the theoretical underpinnings of his approach.

Critics have said that Rogers' approach to therapy is naive and superficial, and although the conditions he describes as necessary and sufficient[4] may be desirable conditions for psychotherapy, they certainly are not *sufficient* for any but mild neurotic problems (Thorne, 1944, 1957; Ellis, 1959; Menninger, 1963; Wolberg, 1967). Thorne, for example, has proposed a strongly eclectic approach to psychotherapy and has criticized Rogers for failing to use diagnosis, for not viewing his therapeutic technique as only one of a large variety of techniques to be used under different conditions, and

[3]From Rogers, C. R. *On becoming a person.* Boston: Houghton Mifflin, 1961. Reprinted by permission.
[4]Briefly, unconditional positive regard (nonpossessive warmth), accurate empathy communicated to the client, therapist congruence or authenticity, client incongruence with his own experience, and contact between therapist and client.

for being naive about the "sick" client's ability to direct the course of therapy. This last point has been made even more strongly by Harper (1959) and by Ellis (1962), both of whom structure therapy in a more cognitively oriented framework, in which the therapist has a strong responsibility for instruction and for rational manipulation of the therapy process.

Perhaps Rogers' most effective answer to the naiveté and superficiality criticisms is that he can provide research evidence that his approach works. More recently, the isolation of the therapeutic conditions and their relations to therapeutic outcome have strengthened his point even further. On the question of whether his approach is useful only with superficial disturbances, Rogers can point to the results of his Wisconsin project (1967) for support —evidence that is somewhat equivocal but better than his critics can provide. For the present discussion, the most interesting result from the Wisconsin project was the finding that although improvement among schizophrenic patients who received psychotherapy was not generally greater than the improvement of patients who did not get therapy, there was evidence that patients who received high levels of congruence, accurate empathy, and positive regard improved on the outcome measures while those who received low levels of these conditions either did not improve or got worse, relative to untreated patients, on the particular measures of outcome used. Rogers would certainly admit that there are methodological shortcomings in nearly all psychotherapy research and that unassailable evidence does not exist. However, the bulk and consistency of the research findings that are accumulating support the efficacy of Rogers' approach and certainly provide better evidence than exists for the views of his critics in most other schools of psychotherapy.

Parenthetically it is worth noting that much of the criticism of client-centered practice has been based on a misunderstanding of the nature of empathy. The communication of accurate empathy is an active rather than a passive process, an issue to be discussed at length later.

Theory. The growing body of research supporting the effectiveness of client-centered therapy helps to answer criticisms of the practice of such therapy. This evidence, however, does not effectively answer the many criticisms leveled against Rogers' theoretical thinking. It is entirely possible to have accurately observed and described effective therapeutic processes and to have developed incorrect explanations of these processes. Rogers' theorizing grew out of his experience as a therapist and did not form the basis for development of his therapeutic techniques.

The most important criticisms of client-centered theory have been attacks on self-actualization as a universal, innate characteristic of human beings. This is one of the most important notions separating humanistic psychologists from psychoanalysts and learning-oriented psychologists. Rogers has made it the most basic and central notion in his explanation of how therapy works, arguing that the therapist's job is to create the right conditions within which the client's self-actualizing tendency can operate to bring about therapeutic growth. The importance of this notion has been well stated by Butler and Rice (1963):

Among psychotherapists, the Rogerians rely most firmly upon growth motivation. Anyone who has observed or heard a competent Rogerian therapist during a therapeutic hour would undoubtedly react negatively to his behavior unless he shared with the therapist the idea that the client has inherent capacities for self-realization. The Rogerian therapist is not a resource for the client, as this concept is usually understood, for he does not give information to the client; he does not provide any new frame of reference from his own store of concepts; he does not impose regimes; and he attempts neither to reassure nor to support the client. He does not manipulate anxiety, acting so as to reduce it when it is too high or increase it when it is too low. Instead he relies in the main upon displaying prizing behavior and communicating his understanding of the client as he presents himself "here and now." It is difficult to imagine a more complete reliance upon the self-restorative capacities of the client than that shown by the Rogerians.

The issue with respect to self-actualizing tendencies, we think, has to do not with their existence but with their origin. Maslow, Goldstein, Rogers, and others think that self-actualizing motives are inherent, basic, and primitive, whereas drive theorists tend to think that self-actualizing motives are based on higher-order reinforcement stemming ultimately from the primary drives and from learnable drives such as fear [p. 81].[5]

[5]From Butler, J. M., & Rice, L. N. Adience, self-actualization, and drive theory. In J. M. Wepman and R. W. Heine (Eds.), *Concepts of personality*. Chicago: Aldine-Atherton, Inc., 1963. Reprinted by permission.

Butler and Rice have set the stage well for a discussion of the self-actualizing tendency. Growth motivation has been postulated as innate by the Rogerians, whereas others have viewed it either as a learned drive or as the capacity to learn. Dollard and Miller (1950), for example, say:

We agree with Rogers that faith in the patient is a most important requirement in a therapist. But we would describe it as a belief in a capacity to
learn rather than one in a capacity to grow because "growth" suggests
physiological models which we do not believe are as appropriate or specific as the principles and conditions of learning. When we affirm the
patient's capacity to learn we mean always "provided the right conditions
are set up." Learning is not inevitable. Our view is better expressed by
the belief that the patient will learn if he must [p. 413].

A similar attack on the conceptual clarity and logical meaning of growth motivation was made by Shoben (1949):

Rogers describes the therapeutic process as a freeing of the "growth
capacities" of the individual, which permits him to acquire "more mature" ways of reacting. If "growth" in this context means (as it must)
something more than physiological maturation and if it is not to be
lumped with the old and rather mystical homeopathic notion of *vis
medicatrix naturae,* it must refer to the client's acquisition of new modes
of response. Such new modes of response are "more mature" because for
a given patient they are less fraught with anxiety or conflict. Thus Rogers
is actually talking about psychotherapy as a learning process [p. 368].

How, the critics ask, does growth motivation work, if not through learning? Surely, they argue, Rogers would not say that mature behaviors are somehow born into the person. At times, though, Rogers does talk of the individual being what he "truly is" and the emergence of the "real self," as though a real self does exist inde-
pendently of the perceived self. Rogers has explicitly rejected the self as an entity, however, and apparent inconsistencies seem to be the result of the literary use of "real self" and similar phrases. Rogers would depend on the "organismic valuing process" to ex-
plain the individual's tendency to choose actualizing alternatives. The critic then would ask how this valuing process works: does this valuing process somehow "know" what is actualizing or are experiences valued by how they "feel"? If the organismic valuing process causes the individual to seek experiences that "feel right," how does this process differ from reinforcement? Many of Rogers' postulates are vaguely worded, and it seems impossible to analyze

them logically without arriving either at a learning position or at a view of some kind of inborn knowledge and decision-making process—requiring a "homunculus" (a kind of person, within the personality, making decisions for the personality). Rogers has explicitly rejected the homunculus notion *and* the learning position (at least in its hard-line, S-R form), making it difficult to formulate his position in a consistent form.

So far I have been dealing with conceptual problems in the notion of self-actualization and have quoted Butler and Rice as saying "the issue with respect to self-actualizing tendencies, we think, has to do not with their existence but with their origin." Many attacks, however, have been made upon the position that self-actualizing tendencies exist at all, or at least that they are universal. These attacks have centered around the argument that the *evidence* for self-actualizing tendencies is either very weak or non-existent. The evidence cited by Rogers for his belief in growth motivation has been based primarily on his clinical experience (he also has cited the general tendency toward growth and differentiation of functioning observed in the process of physical development). He says:

It has been my experience that persons have a basically positive direction. In my deepest contacts with individuals in therapy, even those whose troubles are most disturbing, whose behavior has been most anti-social, whose feelings seem most abnormal, I find this to be true [1961, p. 26].

It is our experience in therapy which has brought us to the point of giving this proposition a central place. The therapist becomes very much aware that the forward moving tendency of the human organism is the basis upon which he relies most deeply and fundamentally. It is evident not only in the general tendency of clients to move in the direction of growth when the factors in the situation are clear; but is most dramatically shown in very serious cases where the individual is on the brink of psychosis or suicide. Here the therapist is very keenly aware that the only force upon which he can basically rely is on the organic tendency toward ongoing growth and enhancement [1951, p. 489].[6]

Some critics have argued that this and similar kinds of evidence (Maslow, 1943; Goldstein, 1940) are based on limited and biased examples. Menninger, for example (1963), has argued that:

[6]Rogers, C. R. *Client-centered therapy*. Boston: Houghton Mifflin, 1951. Reprinted by permission.

Carl Rogers is only half right when he urges his students to recognize that in most if not "all individuals there exist growth forces, tendencies toward self-actualization, which may act as the sole motivation for therapy. We have not realized that under suitable psychological conditions those forces bring about emotional release in those areas and at those rates which are most beneficial to the individual. ... The individual has the capacity and the strength to devise, quite unguided, the steps which will lead him to a more mature and more comfortable relationship to his reality."

This conviction is the cornerstone for Rogers' philosophy and the essential rationale for his "non-directive therapy." The misgivings about this position, expressed by one of us some years ago, bear repetition here. It is the insufficiency of this philosophy as an exclusive rationale for treatment which has made it unpopular in some quarters where concern is felt about the danger that a Pollyannish optimism would interfere with the acceptance of therapeutic responsibility for a patient. Sick individuals differ in the strength and effectiveness of their "drive toward health." In some people the will to live and grow flickers, fades, or even dies. What is it which prevents "release" in some patients of the propensities for progressive adaptation and change? It may reassure the therapist to believe that a patient if left to his own devices in a permissive setting will find the best possible solution to his neurotic predicament. But we all know of patients who under such circumstances seemed to get caught up in an even more relentless self-destructive process leading to still more failures, more suffering, more defeat. Many patients whom we see, seem to have committed themselves, consciously or unconsciously, to stagnation or slow spiritual death [pp. 397–398].[7]

Rogers has depended primarily on his clinical experience for his belief in self-actualizing tendencies, and Menninger has answered that *his* clinical experience has taught him that Rogers' belief is only a half-truth. In addition, Cofer and Appley (1964) have discussed self-actualization as a motivational system and have concluded:

... the evidential basis for these ideas ... is, we think, a limited one. Whether human nature, unspoiled by society, is as satisfactory as these viewpoints lead us to believe is certainly questionable. And it will be difficult either to confirm or to infirm this proposition, on empirical grounds. ... The emphasis on self-actualization ... suffers, in our opinion, from the vagueness of its concepts, the looseness of its language, and the inadequacy of the evidence related to its major contentions. It is difficult to see how it can foster meaningful investigations in view of its vague language [pp. 691–692].

[7]From *The Vital Balance* by Karl Menninger. Copyright © 1963 by Karl Menninger, M.D., The Viking Press, Inc., N. Y. Reprinted by permission.

In summary, the notion of self-actualization has been attacked for being an unclear concept and for being unsupported by evidence. Except among humanistic psychologists, the existence of growth motivation or self-actualizing drives has not been widely accepted.

Butler and Rice (1963), however, have proposed a reinterpretation of growth motivation, which may find wider acceptance. They have based their argument on the now extensive literature supporting the view that exploratory behavior seems somehow to be innately motivated. Butler and Rice suggest:

> that there is a drive—we shall call it *stimulus hunger* or *adient motivation* —which is a primary drive, perhaps even the most pervasive primary drive. We believe that this drive is the primal base for self-actualizing behavior and may be characterized fairly as a developmental drive in the sense that it results in development [p. 82].

By arguing that the organism has an innate need for stimulation, which results in exploratory behavior, Butler and Rice have avoided the theoretical problem of supporting innate teleological, or goal-oriented, behavior. The individual's stimulus hunger motivates him to seek new experience, causing the learning of new and more adaptive behaviors. Exploratory behavior, both in thought and action, results in growth, in self-actualization. When this exploratory behavior is blocked, neurotic problems develop, since the self-actualizing process is stopped; that is, the learning of new and more adaptive behaviors is blocked. Butler and Rice then characterize the job of the psychotherapist as that of facilitating a client's self-experiencing—facilitating his explorations of his own feelings and thoughts—thus permitting new and more adaptive behavior patterns to develop. The key issue, argue Butler and Rice, is that because the client is innately motivated to seek new experience, the therapist can depend on this tendency as a motivating force for therapeutic change. Butler and Rice have substituted stimulus hunger and its consequences for the less defensible notion of self-actualizing tendencies in dealing with the central theoretical issue in client-centered thinking.

In addition to the difficulties surrounding the notion of self-actualizing tendencies, one other widely mentioned theoretical difficulty in Rogers' thinking has to do with the general nature of

phenomenology. Rogers and other phenomenologists have generally rejected learning-theory positions as being too past-oriented
and deterministic. To oversimplify the phenomenological position: the person directs his behavior by choosing the most self-
actualizing alternative among the alternatives available to him.
The phenomenologist explains nonactualized behavior as a case of
a person's misperceiving the alternatives available to him. The
phenomenologists' position is presented as future-oriented and
stresses the individual's control of his own behavior, through what
usually sounds like free choice, in writings of these theorists. The
central difficulty with this thinking is most clearly pointed out by
the question: why does the person misperceive his alternatives?
Or, more generally, why does the person perceive his alternatives
as he does? How does he predict the possible outcomes of the
various behaviors available to him and make his choice accordingly? The answer to these questions most certainly must be some
variant of the position that one's perceptions and anticipated outcomes are based on one's previous experiences with similar
choices. The only alternative is to say that somehow the individual
is born with the knowledge of the consequences of his behavior,
a position that is indefensible. If one's perceptions are indeed
determined by previous experiences, the phenomenological position can be seen as a learning position one step removed; one's
perceptions determine one's behavior and previous experience determines the perceptions. Stated this way, the position is one a
learning therapist could comfortably accept. A critic of
phenomenology might further ask: does the individual ever
choose nonactualizing alternatives *as he perceives the alternatives?* If
the answer is that he does not choose unhealthy alternatives, as
he perceives them, then his behavior is truly determined by his
perceptions. If the answer is that he does sometimes choose unhealthy alternatives, as he perceives them, the phenomenologist is
faced with having to explain why the individual violates his self-
actualizing tendency. (See the discussion of this issue in Patterson,
1966.)

These critical comments on Rogers have established an interesting
dilemma. There is considerable evidence that Rogers' approach to
therapy is effective. His theoretical position, however, is open to
serious attack and has not found wide acceptance among the
scientific community. A major purpose of this book is to resolve
some of that dilemma.

Learning: Interview therapy

Dollard and Miller (1950) have had an extensive influence in the areas of personality development and psychotherapy. Criticisms of their position have included attacks on their theoretical basis, on the usefulness of the techniques they have described, and on the lack of research supporting their discussion of psychotherapy. Their influence has probably been most pervasive and effective in the area of personality development. Our interest here, however, is in their treatment of psychotherapy.

Theory. The hard-line drive-reductionist position is that drive reduction accounts for all learning. This position has been widely criticized, and in later writings Miller has recognized the probability that drive reduction would have to be abandoned in its "hard" form (1959). Miller's feeling is that other principles of learning may be discovered but that drive reduction is the best explanation available at present. Drive reduction still has a powerful following and support (Brown, 1961), but its critics are many. In an important work, Cofer and Appley (1964) have questioned the ubiquitous nature of drive reduction, but even their position involves an emphasis on drive-like variables (Siegel, 1965). Shoben (1949), another major influence on learning-oriented interview therapy, did not base his discussion of psychotherapy on drive-reduction theory, but rather adopted Mowrer's two-factor learning theory and arrived at approximately the same position on psychotherapy as Dollard and Miller. Dollard and Miller have argued that their discussion of psychotherapy could fit comfortably within any of a number of specific learning theories. Most of their discussion is not based on the specific process by which learning takes place but on such well-demonstrated processes as generalization, conflict, and reinforcement (without reference to drive reduction). Other learning-oriented psychotherapists have also based their ideas on a soft-line learning-theory position (Rotter, 1954).

A second line of criticism concerns whether or not personality is learned, to the extent that Dollard and Miller argue it is. (It should be noted that Dollard and Miller presented their arguments as hypotheses to be confirmed or disconfirmed by research.) Some have argued (Amsel, 1961) that stable higher-order conditioning has been difficult to demonstrate experimentally and that this may weaken the usefulness of the notion of secondary drives. The learning theorist would reply that, throughout life, first-order conditioning and primary drives continue to be involved in learning experiences, which are based on extremely complicated patterns of *both* secondary and primary drive reduction. In addition, the learning approach to personality development has inspired such an extensive research literature, which is generally confirmatory, that it would be difficult to argue with the position that what we call personality is primarily the result of learning. Recent applications of this position to personality development and psychopathology can be found in Lundin (1969) and Maher (1966). It also seems clear that the learning approach to neurosis has been the most extensively validated and seems to represent the most prominent trend for the future of psychotherapy. (Chapter 3 discusses this approach to neurosis more thoroughly.)

Practice. Comments on the therapy techniques proposed by Dollard and Miller have varied widely. Raimy (1952) said that Dollard and Miller presented:

one of the best descriptions in the literature of the most generally accepted techniques, admonitions, and rules of thumb found in the practice of almost all psychotherapists. . . . The second half could almost be used alone as an introduction to the principles of psychotherapy. Despite its definite psychoanalytic orientation, probably few psychotherapists will quarrel much with the general contents.

James Miller and John Butler (1952), however, contended that:

despite the title of the book [*Personality and Psychotherapy*], they did not associate their notions with psychotherapy in general. Rather they produced a book limited to the special case of prolonged psychoanalysis. Freudian theory and Freudian descriptions of therapeutic situations have at times been substituted for actual observations. Such a formulation leaves little room for other schools of treatment unless it explains their effectiveness in psychoanalytic terms or dismisses them as ineffectual [p. 183].

While applauding Dollard and Miller's conceptual clarity, Ford and Urban (1963) commented that:

this system cannot stand alone as a treatment procedure. By this, we mean that a practitioner could not pick up the volume *Personality and Psychother-*

apy and proceed to practice techniques of verbal therapy. Although he would have a rationale by which to account for the general ways in which responses can be connected with other responses and to situational events, he would find scant information about which responses are likely to be encountered in what conditions, what kinds of responses are likely to be related to which other ones ... and the like [p. 272].

This last statement points out what is probably the most important criticism of Dollard and Miller's book as a work on psychotherapy; from the rationale the authors provide, a therapist could find justification for whatever techniques he wishes. Incompatible approaches, for example, are described as appropriate "under different conditions." Dollard and Miller say that the patient should be permitted to make his own discoveries and hit upon his own verbal labels if he is able to do so; if not, the therapist should intervene and provide the labels. However, an authoritarian therapist could justify his quick intervention, whereas a more passive therapist would offer the same rationale for a vastly different approach. Also, the therapist is counseled not to judge and criticize, but he is encouraged to point out shortcomings, contradictions, and inappropriate verbalizations in the patient's story. By most standards these latter messages are considered judgmental or critical, and Dollard and Miller do not specify how they are to be communicated in a nonjudgmental way.

This ambiguity is perhaps one of the reasons why few therapists consider themselves "followers" of Dollard and Miller in terms of therapeutic practice. Another reason is that learning-oriented therapists—the potential "followers"—are rapidly identifying with the behavior-modification approach.

Research. In a review of *Personality and Psychotherapy,* Raimy (1952) predicted that:

one can expect a "rash" of new research to be aimed directly at the clearly stated principles which these authors espouse. Adequate research designs that deal directly with patients undergoing treatment will, as always, be developed by only a few and with the greatest of difficulty [p. 344].

The second part of Raimy's prediction has unfortunately been more than borne out. Dollard and Miller's ideas have inspired extensive research in the area of personality development but not in the area of psychotherapy.

One important exception to this statement is a series of four dissertations done at Pennsylvania State University and reported by Ashby, Ford, Guerney, and Guerney (1957). In a laudable attempt to deal with the difficult problems of experimental control in therapy research, these authors trained their therapists to perform "reflective" therapy with half of their patients and "leading" (more directive) therapy with the other half. The reflective approach was based primarily on Rogers' writings, and the therapists were instructed to:

create a warm, acceptant, understanding, noncritical psychological atmosphere; to understand and accept the feelings which the client experiences as a result of his perceptions; and to communicate this acceptance and understanding to the client. . . . It is necessary for the therapist to accept and clarify only those thoughts and feelings which the therapist believes are in the client's present phenomenological field. These thoughts and feelings must be strongly implied by the client himself, if they are not explicitly communicated either verbally or nonverbally.

In contrast, "leading" therapy was based primarily on the writings of Dollard and Miller and of Fromm-Reichmann (1950). In this approach, the therapists were encouraged:

to create a warm, accepting, understanding, noncritical psychological atmosphere; to contrast the client's report of his situation and difficulties with an objective reality as the therapist deduces it; to formulate hypotheses about the defenses which protect the conflicts; and to intervene in such a way that he helps the client understand the nature and function of the defenses. The therapist may then help the client in coping directly with underlying conflicts at a level which the therapist deems advisable and feasible within the limitations of time and the client's personal dynamics. He thus helps the client to become reoriented in terms of reality. . . . It is necessary for the therapist to introduce, or direct attention to, factors not within the client's present awareness, in order to make the client aware of his defenses, to help him modify them or eliminate the need for them, to recognize his conflicts, emotional reactions, and needs, and to bring the client to adopt alternative patterns of perception and behavior.

Many outcome and process measures were examined and a number of interesting variables were discussed in detail. Comparisons of the two therapy approaches, however, yielded equivocal results. Analyses indicated significant differences between the approaches on only two measures: the clients of reflective therapists demonstrated less verbal guardedness in the first four interviews, and the therapists' post-therapy rating of improvement favored the effectiveness of the directive approach. The authors point out that this last finding is difficult to interpret, since all but one of the therapists expressed a preference for the directive approach prior to the beginning of the experiment. The possibility of a rating bias obviously existed.

The discouraging fact seems to be that a body of research comparable to client-centered research has not developed, either to support or contradict the efficacy of the approach to therapy proposed by Dollard and Miller, Shoben, and other learning theorists oriented toward interview psychotherapy.

Behavior modification

Judging from the volume of material being published by behavior modifiers, from the number of training institutes being established, and from the increase in university psychology programs in behavior modification, this approach is clearly becoming one of the most important influences in the therapy field. The movement has attracted vocal support and vocal criticism, and, as in previous sections, the approach can be discussed in terms of theory, clinical application, and research.

Theory. The critics of behavior-modification theory range from those who reject learning approaches generally (Breger and McGaugh, 1965; Weitzman, 1967) to learning-oriented psychologists who have suggested that some behavior modifiers' (Wolpe, 1958) neuropsychology is not well founded (Rotter, 1959) and that the behavior modifiers' view of neurosis is simplistic and oriented toward specific symptoms (Goodstein, 1967). Rotter has also mentioned a few of the points to be discussed in Chapter 3, such as the behavior modifiers' lack of discussion of internalized conflicts. Rotter notes, for example, that Wolpe does not explain "why [feared] stimuli may be ever present in thought" (1958, p. 177). Such an explanation would probably be similar to Shoben's discussion of internalized conflicts (1949; Shaffer & Shoben, 1956; also see Chapter 3). In fact, behavior modifiers' descriptions of neurosis differ from those of other learning theorists in a number of ways. In general, most psychologists who adopt a learning view would agree that neurotic behavior is learned, and that it is learned according to the same principles by which normal behavior is learned. Beyond this general agreement, however, some learning-oriented psychologists adopt a more complicated view of neurosis than many behavior modifiers seem to adopt. Behavior modifiers, for example, usually discuss neurosis in terms of external cues and seem not to deal with the issue of internalized conflict—an issue that occupies a very important place in the literature on anxiety. In many ways, this external-cue orientation seems to lead to a "phobia orientation" among the behavior modifiers, most of whom suggest that phobias are the clearest examples of directly conditioned fears and anxieties. As I will argue in Chapter 3, phobias often have an etiology quite different from that of directly conditioned fears.

Generally, the epithet thrown at behavior modifiers has been "Too simplistic!" There was some truth to this criticism in the early writings, but the accuracy of the criticism seems to be diminishing as behavior modifiers' theoretical analyses become more complex. Hunt and Dyrud (1968) have commented that success will ultimately depend on "how well this behavioristic approach can avoid entrapment in simplistic analysis" (p. 143).

Practice. Criticisms of the techniques employed by behavior modifiers center around the observation that a simplistic view of neurosis leads to a simplistic view of treatment. Critics see behavior-modification techniques as superficial and incomplete. They suggest that behavior modifiers frequently violate the limits of their own techniques and that they have recently moved toward a wide variety of therapeutic approaches, many of which are quite similar to traditional approaches. One recent article resulted from a visit by a number of psychoanalytically oriented therapists to a clinic where Wolpe and Lazarus were working (Klein, Dittmann, Parloff, & Gill, 1969). Their article is an interesting series of observations, interspersed with rebuttal comments by Wolpe and Lazarus. The trend of their observations is that behavior therapists actually perform therapy in a more complicated manner than is implied in their writings. The wide variety of techniques attempted by Wolpe and Lazarus include "a good deal of indoctrination, teaching, and exhortation." Breger and McGaugh (1965) also point out that much of what has actually happened in the cases reported by behavior therapists cannot be directly related to learning techniques. Much time is spent in traditional interview sessions, and it is clear that, in most cases, a relationship between the therapist and patient exists, making it impossible to assign any therapeutic gains solely to the behavior-modification techniques used. They suggest that this broadening of techniques beyond the stated ones is made necessary by the fact that few neurotic problems actually fit the phobia and/or specific-symptom model. They cite one informal survey in which about 3% of clinic patients exhibit such symptoms, and others have commented that phobias and/or specific-symptom-type neuroses make up a small percentage of the patient population of clinics and private practitioners (Klein, Dittmann, Parloff, & Gill, 1969).

Behavior modifiers do seem to be moving toward a greater complexity of treatment approaches, as is indicated by Franks' (1969) advocacy of "total behavioral management," in which the therapist is not so narrow that "he focuses upon the presenting symptom and ignores the rest of the person" (p. 17). Lazarus (1967) has recommended "broad-spectrum behavior therapy" and "technical eclecticism," in which he seems to be advocating the pragmatic application of any technique that works. The danger in such an atheoretical shotgun approach has been commented on by Wolpe, however (1968). Blind empiricism could cause the loss of the learning basis of behavior modification and lead to confusion and a slowing of progress, but we can expect the complexity of behavior-modification treatment to continue to increase.

Research. Much of the early popularity and influence of behavior therapy was no doubt due to its claims for superior effectiveness and quicker functioning. This initial enthusiasm was based in large part on evidence reported by Wolpe (1958), who claimed that 90% of the neurotics treated with behavior therapy could be classified as improved. This rate was compared with the frequently referred-to improvement rate of 60–70% in psychoanalysis. In recent years, Wolpe has been criticized (Stevenson, 1964) for reporting the data in the manner he did, since his research was vulnerable to reporting bias (the roles of therapist, researcher, and outcome test administrator overlapped). Perhaps more importantly, a selection bias was used, so that *some* patients who received fewer than 15 interviews were judged (by the therapist-researcher) not to have received a "sufficient amount" of the treatment approach. All patients who completed at least 15 sessions were included in Wolpe's statistics. This procedure obviously biased the results strongly in favor of the treatment technique, and Stevenson has pointed out that, had Wolpe not discarded these patients, his improvement rate would also have been approximately 65%.

Since Wolpe's early studies, the behavior-modification approach has inspired a large body of research. Much of it has been laboratory research involving the modification of specific animal (snakes, rats, spiders) fears in otherwise normal subjects (Lang & Lazovik, 1963; Lang, 1965; Cooke, 1966; Davison, 1968; Rachman, 1965, 1966a, 1966b; Shannon & Wolff, 1967; Bandura & Menlove, 1968). Such laboratory "analogies" to therapy have both advantages and disadvantages, but there is considerable question about the appropriateness of viewing animal fears as analogous to neurosis, since the former seem to be directly conditioned fears, whereas neurosis involves internalized and/or displaced fears. Several studies on neurosis-like anxiety have attempted to maintain experimental control with human subjects. These studies have dealt with the fear of taking tests (Johnson, 1966; Emery & Krumboltz, 1967; Katahn, Strenger, & Cherry, 1966); with "social anxiety" (college students who volunteered themselves as socially anxious, excluding those who needed psychiatric care—Rehm & Marston, 1968); and, in Gordon Paul's elegantly designed series of studies, with the fear of public speaking (1966, 1967, 1968). Paul compared the results of systematic desensitization, "insight" therapy, attention placebo, and no treatment. The desensitization treatment was superior to all other treatments, and the "insight" therapy and attention placebo were superior to no treatment. In addition, those treated with systematic desensitization maintained their gains over a long follow-up period, and the benefits of their increased social skill seemed to generalize to other areas of functioning.

Behavior modification has established an impressive research record in the treatment of well-specified fears and, to some extent, anxieties with relatively clear precipitants. Hospital programs have also demonstrated some positive results. What is lacking is well-designed research on the treatment of "central life problems" (Paul, 1969), of the kind typically seen in the outpatient clinic. The nearest approach to such a study has been Paul and Shannon's (1966) treatment of social-evaluative anxiety in group systematic desensitization.

Neurotic problems for which people seek therapy seldom have clear precipitants, and the major criticism of behavior modification has been that it is too simplified for the treatment of complex problems. Laboratory analogue simplifications represent useful research strategy, but they are not sufficient to establish behavior modification as a *replacement* for interview psychotherapy. (I will argue later that behavior modification is an appropriate supplement to interview therapy.) We might expect some clinical research of at least the sophistication level of the early client-centered research (Rogers and Dymond, 1954). Unfortunately, most clinical studies have included considerable contamination of research design, of the kind in Wolpe's early research (Lazarus, 1961).

Beyond these studies, much of the evidence for behavior therapy has been based on case histories and on clinical studies that do not embody control procedures. It is discouraging that a therapeutic approach so explicitly based on experimental evidence has not resulted in a large-scale clinical study or even in a series of smaller, well-controlled studies of self-referred patients. The number of case histories of successful treatment reported by behavior modifiers is very impressive and probably indicates the potential validity of the approach, but the support of an approach to psychotherapy can no longer be based primarily on case histories. That strategy belongs to the past. For one thing, case histories are quite vulnerable to observer and selection bias, and they are not sufficiently controlled for proof of efficacy or for the systematic improvement of our approach to psychotherapy. It is probably only a matter of time before laboratory research and case histories are joined by well-designed research in outpatient clinics.

By now my bias should be very clear. The influence of psychoanalysis seems to be on the wane. Its influence on the practice of psychotherapy has been enormous, but its theoretical basis seems no longer tenable, and evidence of its effectiveness as an approach to treatment has failed to emerge. The writings of individual analysts contain valuable contributions, and these will continue to have an influence on the practice of therapy—but not as a unified system with which large numbers of therapists will identify. In later chapters I will make frequent reference to some of these contributions. Client-centered therapy had an initial period of great influence but has been somewhat less influential in recent years—with one major exception: researchers have continued to report evidence for the effectiveness of Rogers' "therapeutic triad"

—accurate empathy, warmth, and congruence. The phenomeno-logical theory of this approach continues to have an extensive following but seems to be open to serious question on a number of grounds. In sum, client-centered therapy appears to work, but its theoretical underpinnings are weak. Other humanistic approaches have enjoyed a recent increase in popularity, especially as a part of the sensitivity-group, awareness-encounter movement. Public attention is not a good criterion for the effectiveness of a therapy approach, however, and it is difficult to make predictions about humanistic approaches in the absence of research evidence, other than that available on client-centered therapy. Gestalt therapy, however (Perls, Hefferline, & Goodman, 1951; Fagan & Shepherd, 1970), is a humanistic approach that may have a unique and increasing influence. Most of the same criticisms that were leveled against Rogers' theorizing apply to the humanistic-phenomenological theories of other humanists. Dollard and Miller have made many significant contributions to the understanding of personality development and the nature of neurosis, but their approach to psychotherapy seems to have faded. The science of psychology appears to be moving in the direction of a general-learning approach, however, and Dollard and Miller's formulation of neurosis is the one that has best stood the test of research. Behavior modification has rapidly acquired an extensive following and is influencing a growing number of graduate programs in clinical psychology. A large number of case histories have reported successful applications of behavior modification in complex neurotic problems, but the same can be said for psychoanalysis. Research evidence for the effectiveness of behavior modification with outpatient neurotic problems has been very sparse but may emerge during the seventies. The early writings of behavior modifiers seemed to present an oversimplified view of the nature of neurosis, in spite of earlier, more complex views presented by others within the learning-theory framework. A trend toward greater complexity, both in theory and practice, makes it likely that behavior modification will be one of the most significant approaches to therapy in the future.

These are my views of the status of the various schools of therapy. Now I will develop what I hope is an internally consistent and useful theoretical model of neurosis and therapy, to form the basis of a systematically eclectic approach.

3

Conflict and neurosis

An understanding of therapy demands an understanding of the principles by which neurotic problems develop. My theoretical model and systematically eclectic approach has developed directly from a view of neurosis as involving all or some of the following characteristics: (1) painful emotions such as anxiety, guilt, and depression, (2) low self-esteem, (3) impaired problem-solving ability, and (4) self-defeating behaviors (which, reluctantly following tradition, I will call "symptoms"). They develop according to the principles of learning and are based primarily on conflict. Conflict can be defined as the tendency to perform two or more incompatible responses at the same time, and this notion is central to the understanding of neurotic behavior. Conflict will be discussed in some detail, followed by an extensive description of the learning view of neurosis. Some of the material on conflict will be familiar to many readers, but since it underlies neurotic problems generally, and since my theoretical model is built on Miller's conflict model, I will risk boring some readers for the sake of completeness.

33

This chapter represents a contemporary version of the learning theories of neurosis as pioneered by Dollard, Miller, and Shoben.

Conflict

Dollard and Miller (1950) say that "an intense emotional conflict is the necessary basis for neurotic behavior" (p. 129). The study of conflict in experimental psychology has been closely associated with Miller's name (1944; 1948; 1959; Miller & Kraeling, 1952; Miller & Murray, 1952), and since his analysis of the dynamics of conflict is basic to the understanding of neurotic behavior, I will deal with this issue in some detail.

Four general types of conflict have been described. *Approach-approach* conflict refers to the situation in which the organism has a tendency to approach separate goals, with the approach of one goal resulting in the loss of the other. A typical example of this type of conflict would be a young woman with two equally attractive suitors, both of whom she wishes to marry; choosing one necessarily results in the loss of the other. This kind of conflict is usually easily resolved, since something usually happens to "tip the balance," making one of the alternatives more desirable than the other. *Avoidance-avoidance* conflict refers to the situation in which two objects or goals elicit fear responses, but the avoidance of one forces movement toward the other. This kind of conflict is exemplified by the student who dislikes and/or fears studying and at the same time fears failing his examination. Avoiding one feared "object" forces an approach to the other, providing a conflict less easily resolved than the approach-approach conflict. Its resolution often requires "leaving the field"; for example, if the student's conflict is strong enough, his solution may be to drop out of school and find a job. The third kind of conflict, *approach-avoidance* conflict, is considerably more devastating than the first two, for it occurs when a particular goal is both desired and feared at the same time. Approach-avoidance conflict has been studied in great detail and has been demonstrated to have debilitating effects on behavior, both in the laboratory and in less formal descriptions of human behavior. An example of an approach-avoidance conflict is a young child who has a punitive mother on whom he is nevertheless totally dependent for love and affection. He cannot avoid his mother because of his dependence on her, yet he cannot approach her because of his fear of her. Another example might be a young woman who both wants marriage and fears it at the same time. The fourth kind of conflict, *double approach-avoidance,* is an elaboration of simple approach-avoidance conflicts, which probably exists only in the laboratory. In life most of our conflicts are intertwined, becoming multiple or double approach-avoidance conflicts, exemplified by our young woman who both wants and fears marriage and who must choose between two equally attractive (and equally feared) suitors.

The devastating effect of approach-avoidance and double approach-avoidance conflicts results from the fact that they are inescapable by their very nature. Except under unusual conditions of restraint, the individual can resolve an avoidance-avoidance or approach-approach conflict. In the case of approach-avoidance conflicts, however, there is "no place to run." When the organism is in a state of conflict, he is in a state of strong and unpleasant arousal. Conflict is a form of frustration, and frustration has been shown to arouse high levels of drive and distinctive internal responses of an aversive nature.

Miller (Dollard & Miller, 1950) analyzes approach-avoidance conflict with the following four principles or assumptions:

1. The tendency to approach a goal is stronger the nearer the subject is to it. This will be called the *gradient of approach.*

This gradient of approach is represented by the solid line in Figure 3–1. The tendency to approach a desired object or goal increases with nearness to the goal because of the *gradient of reinforcement;* the cues immediately surrounding the goal are the most reinforcing and therefore elicit the strongest approach response. As one gets farther from the goal the cues become less similar to the goal and therefore elicit weaker approach responses. The less similar the cues, the less the response generalizes. In Miller's work and in subsequent studies of conflict, "nearness" to the goal is determined by physical proximity as well as other dimensions. For example, if a subject in an experiment were conditioned to have approach responses for a red light, the approach responses would also be elicited by a pink light, and the darker the pink color, the more strongly would the response be elicited. In this situation, the subject is approaching the red light not through space but along the dimension of *stimulus similarity.* In addition to the dimensions of physical proximity and stimulus similarity, an organism can approach a goal along the dimension of *time.* As the time for a desired response approaches, the tendency to perform the response increases.

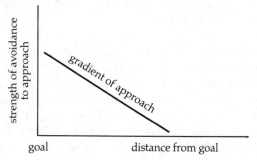

Figure 3–1. The approach gradient. The tendency to approach a goal is stronger the nearer the subject is to the goal.

2. The tendency to avoid a feared stimulus is stronger the nearer the subject is to it. This will be called the *gradient of avoidance.*

Again because of stimulus generalization, the closer one is to a feared object, the more strongly the fear response will be elicited. The gradient of avoidance is represented by the dotted line in Figure 3–2.

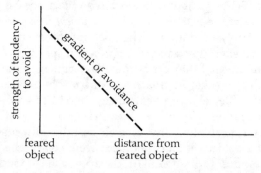

Figure 3–2. The avoidance gradient. The tendency to avoid a feared object is stronger the nearer the subject is to the object.

3. The strength of avoidance increases more rapidly with nearness than does that of approach. In other words, the gradient of avoidance is *steeper* than that of approach.

This principle is illustrated by Figure 3–3, in which Figures 3–1 and 3–2 have been superimposed upon each other. If a goal is the object of approach-avoidance conflict, it will be both desired and feared at the same time. (Such a goal is referred to as a *feared goal.*) As a subject approaches a feared goal, both his fear and approach responses increase in strength, but the fear response increases more rapidly. When the subject is still far from the feared goal, his approach tendency may be stronger than his avoidance tendency and he will engage in approach behavior. But as he comes nearer to the goal, the strength of the fear response may catch up with the approach response so that the approach and avoidance tendencies will be equal in strength. This point is represented in Figure 3–3 as the place where the gradients cross and is the point at which behavior should stop, with the subject in a state of conflict.

Figure 3–3. Approach-avoidance conflict. Both approach and avoidance tendencies increase with nearness to a feared goal, but avoidance increases faster; that is, the avoidance gradient is steeper. Behavior will vacillate between approach and avoidance at the point where the gradients cross. (From Dollard, J. & Miller, N. E. *Personality and psychotherapy: An analysis in terms of learning, thinking, and culture,* 1950. Used with permission of McGraw-Hill Book Company.)

4. The strength of the tendencies to approach or to avoid varies with the strength of the drive upon which they are based. In other words, an increase in drive raises the height of the entire gradient.

Figure 3–3 might represent the conflict of a young man who desperately wants to date girls yet at the same time is desperately afraid of contact with them. When he is far from a date, perhaps on a Monday, he might engage in approach behavior and ask a girl for a date the following weekend. As the feared goal approaches, however, his fear responses increase in strength to the point where they are equal to and then stronger than his approach responses. By Thursday, perhaps, his avoidance tendencies are stronger than his approach tendencies and he cancels the date.

An understanding of principle four suggests a number of ways his conflict might be resolved. Figure 3–4a illustrates the condition in which the drive behind his approach tendencies is increased. His social-sexual needs become stronger and raise the height of the entire approach gradient so that the approach response is always stronger than the avoidance response. Figure 3–4b illustrates the case in which the conflicted young man has had a number of rewarding experiences with girls and his fear response has been weakened by counterconditioning. The height of his avoidance gradient has been lowered. In this case, even though his approach tendency is of the same strength as before, it is at all times stronger than his avoidance tendency. A third possibility (Figure 3–4c) is that recurring, severely painful experiences with girls might strengthen his fear response to the extent that his avoidance tendencies are always stronger than his approach tendencies, causing him to avoid girls but not to be in conflict about doing so (an unlikely but possible circumstance).

Although modifications of this formulation of the dynamics of conflict have been proposed (Maher, 1966), Miller's analysis has received widespread experimental support and has played an important part in increasing our understanding of neurosis. Phillips (1956) has gone so far as to say, "There is no psychopathology without conflict" (p. 127). This is probably too extreme a statement, but it seems safe to say that without conflict there is no anxiety-based psychopathology (psychopathic behavior, for example, might be based on too little anxiety rather than on too much). Conflict results in remarkably persistent strong emotional responses that generalize to previously neutral stimuli, and Shaffer and Shoben (1956) describe the experience of conflict as one of helpless anxiety. An understanding of conflict probably provides the clearest distinction between fear and anxiety. Both fear and anxiety seem to be derivatives of pain and are therefore the same experience in many ways. They are distinguishable in individuals'

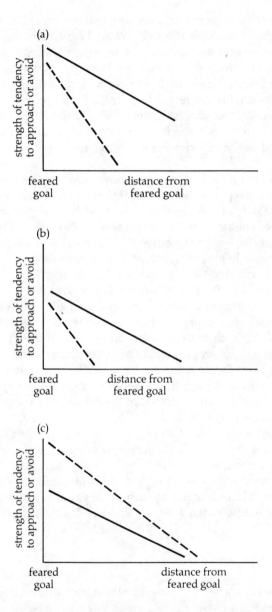

Figure 3–4. Different means of conflict resolution. (a) Strengthening the approach tendency. (b) Weakening the avoidance tendency. (c) Strengthening the avoidance tendency to the point where it is stronger than approach at all times.

reports of their experiences, however, and are related to differing physiological responses (Cattell, 1963). Two traditional distinctions between fear and anxiety are that (1) the cues for fear are specific and known, whereas cues for anxiety are unrecognized by the anxious individual; and (2) anxiety is more of an apprehension than a fear—that is, anxiety is fear with a future referent. Perhaps more basically, fear can be understood as a directly conditioned aversive reaction to a specific cue, whereas anxiety can best be understood as the experience most often associated with conflict.

Personality theorists with a clinical orientation and experimentalists both have seen conflict as central to their theoretical positions. Freud (1935), for example, saw tension within the personality as the result of conflict between driving forces and restraining forces. Jung (1953) also assigned a central position to the conflict of these forces, although he conceived of the forces within personality differently. Horney (1945) assigned "inner conflicts" a central place in her theorizing, and Rogers (1959) stressed conflict between the "organismic valuing process" and the "self concept." Experimental approaches to conflict include Pavlov's (1941) experiments in which dogs were conditioned to approach either a circle or an ellipse and to avoid the other shape. When the two geometric figures were altered to be so similar that they could not be discriminated, the resulting discrimination-induced approach-avoidance conflict caused disorganized behavior in the dogs. The work of Miller (1944, 1951, 1959), Brown (1948, 1957, 1961), and many others has provided an explicit, well-documented literature on the nature of conflict and other forms of frustration; a summary of this literature is available in Yates (1962). Worell (1967) reports a number of studies describing the effect of conflict on humans, in which he relates conflicts to such factors as intrapersonal instability, originality, moral training, and the generalization of conflict.

The neurotic paradox

Some behaviors seem to cause unnecessary suffering for an individual and can therefore be termed "neurotic" behaviors. Another criterion for describing behavior as neurotic is that it be indiscriminate; that is, an individual behaves in ways that may have been appropriate in a previous setting but are not appropriate in his present circumstances. Both these statements lead us to the general definition of neurotic or maladaptive behaviors as those that are self-defeating or self-punitive.

The learning theorist is faced with an apparent paradox if he speaks of behavior as self-punitive. It becomes difficult to reconcile the existence of self-punitive behavior with the idea of reinforcement maintaining all behavior. Why would behavior with negative consequences for the individual be reinforced? Attempts to understand this apparent paradox have resulted in several experimental studies that have enhanced the understanding of neurotic behavior.

A classic animal study done by Farber (1948) remains one of the best experimental illustrations of how self-punitive behavior is maintained.[1] Farber ran rats through a T-maze like the one pictured in Figure 3–5. Farber's animals were all fed just enough to keep them hungry and were all run through 40 learning trials in which each rat ran from the start box to one or the other of the arms of the maze where food was provided. Each rat always was fed in the same arm of the maze and developed a well-learned response of running to that goal box. After 40 learning trials, half of the animals were assigned to a control condition and permitted to perform 60 more trials exactly like the learning trials. The other half of the animals were submitted to the following procedure: the animal had to cross an electrically charged grid to get to the food; if he chose the other arm of the maze, he also had to cross an electric grid, but he received no food. If an animal refused to run to either of the goal boxes, shock was administered through the separate grid in the main alley. The animal was also prevented from returning to the start box, so it had to make a choice and run to one of the goal boxes. After several learning trials each of the animals learned to turn, run across the grid, and receive the food in the goal box. Like the control animals the experimental group had 60 trials during this phase of the experiment. Farber reported a number of interesting findings, but the one of greatest interest to us is that in the third phase of the experiment all shocks were

[1]There is danger in generalizing inappropriately from animal studies to human behavior. Many principles, however, are better illustrated by animal studies, in which researchers can exercise greater experimental control. When I refer to animal studies I will also try to give related examples of human behavior.

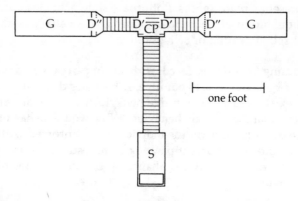

Figure 3–5. Floor plan of Farber's T-maze. S—starting box; CP—choice point; G—goal box; D—door; dotted line in front of door—curtain; shaded area—grid. (From Farber, I. E. Response fixation under anxiety and nonanxiety conditions. *Journal of Experimental Psychology,* April 1948, **38** (2), 117. By permission of the author and the American Psychological Association.)

discontinued, and the food was provided in the arm of the maze opposite the one to which each animal was accustomed to running. The animals who had received no shocks required an average of approximately 10 trials to learn to change their choice and run to the opposite goal box to receive the food. The animals who had run across the electrified grid to reach their food required an average of over 60 trials to learn to turn in the opposite direction and receive their food, even though no shocks were being administered. By continuing to run to the original goal box, the experimental animals seemed to exhibit self-punitive or maladaptive behavior. When we examine this apparently unreinforced behavior, we see that, at the choice point, the experimental animals were in a strong approach-avoidance conflict; they had a tendency both to run to the food and to avoid running across the electric grid. The choice point thus became associated with a strongly aversive state of arousal. The experiment was designed so that the only behavior that would reduce this aversive arousal was running rapidly toward the goal box containing the food. Subsequently, even when the electricity was turned off, the cues surrounding the choice point had acquired a strongly aversive nature—that is, they were anxiety arousing. In the past the behavior that had reduced similar anxiety was running toward the goal box in which the food was originally placed. *Anxiety and fear reduction are extremely strong rein-forcers.* Apparently, Farber's animals had been so strongly rein-forced for the behavior of running to the original goal box that even the absence of food (itself a frustrating or punishing condi-tion) was not strong enough to prevent the maintenance of a now "neurotic" behavior.

One simple example of analogous behavior in humans might be a child who is so terrified of being alone that he acts obnoxious to gain attention in the present moment, thus relieving his im-mediate fear but at great cost in the future, since he soon will have no friends. We will see many other more complex and meaningful examples throughout this book.

More recent studies with animals have demonstrated similar effects under somewhat different conditions (Brown, Martin, & Morrow, 1964; Brown, 1965; Martin & Moon, 1968; Beecroft & Brown, 1967; Beecroft, Bouska, & Fisher, 1967; Beecroft, 1967; Beecroft & Bouska, 1967). In these experiments rats were trained to run down a 6-foot alley from a start box to a goal box in order to avoid electric shock in the start box and alley (see Figure 3–6). After this behavior was well established, control animals were placed in the start box and administered no shock in the apparatus. At first they tended to run to the goal box, but soon this behavior extinguished and they stopped running or ran more slowly. Ex-perimental animals, however, were shocked in the alley but not in the start box. (In some studies shocks were administered through-out the alley and in others in only part of the alley; in some studies the alley was electrified on every trial and in other studies was electrified on only some of the trials.) The consistent finding of interest to our discussion is that experimental animals continued to run to the goal box for many more trials and at faster rates, even though they could have avoided shock entirely by staying in the start box. The most likely explanation of these findings is that among the experimental animals fear reduction had so strongly reinforced the running behavior that they left the start box and began running before sufficient extinction of the fear response had time to occur. They then ran across the shock, further arousing their fear and, upon entering the goal box, were strongly rein-forced for their running behavior by fear reduction, even on the extinction trials. (It is relevant to note that considerable pilot work is required to determine the effective dimensions of the apparatus in experiments like these. If the alley, for example, had been considerably longer the experimental animals might not have reached the electrified grid before their responses began to extinguish significantly.)

Scale: ½" = 1'

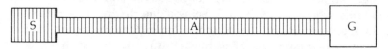

Figure 3–6. Brown's apparatus for the learning of self-punitive running. Floor plan: S is the start box into which the rats were dropped; A is the six-foot alley leading to G, the goal box, which is the only area that did not have an electric grid floor.

These experiments establish two important principles. The most relevant point, obviously, is that what appears to be *self-punitive behavior is established and maintained by the powerfully reinforcing effects of fear or anxiety reduction.* A second important principle is that *fear persists because the organism is motivated to avoid feared cues so rapidly that relearning cannot take place.* I will make frequent use of this observation later.

Again at the level of simple analogy, these principles might be illustrated by a girl who is in conflict over wanting intimate relationships and fearing them at the same time. Her avoidance behavior might be to become involved in relationships up to a certain point and then to become suddenly vicious and drive the other person away. Her viciousness, although it is ultimately self-defeating, brings immediate relief from her fear of intimacy and therefore is strongly reinforced. This well-established avoidance behavior also prevents her from ever being intimate, so she can never relearn her responses to the fear of intimacy. The fear will not simply disappear; it must be relearned in the presence of whatever is feared. All of these events are further complicated by the fact that she is not aware of many of her motives and the causes of many of her fears. Understanding how such a complicated situation can develop is our task in the rest of this chapter.

The animal studies discussed help clarify the principles involved in self-punitive behavior, and these principles have been applied

to human behavior in an experiment reported by Stone and Hokanson (1969). In this study each subject was seated in front of a
panel on which three response buttons appeared, prominently
labeled "point," "shock," and "self-shock." The subject was led
to believe that another subject (actually an experimental confeder-
ate) was also seated in front of a similar panel. Electrodes were
fastened to the back of the subject's left hand, and he was told that
the purpose of the experiment was to study a situation "analogous
to 'real life' interpersonal affairs wherein people frequently have
the options of hurting someone else (shock), being friendly
(point), or 'taking it out' on oneself (self-shock)." When the subject pushed the button labeled "point," he was indicating his
desire to give a small reward to his "fellow-subject." When he
pushed the button marked "shock," he thought he was shocking
his "fellow-subject," and when he pushed the button marked
"self-shock," he administered a shock to himself which had been
calibrated to be at 3/4 the intensity of shock that he considered
painful. The experiment itself consisted of three phases. In the first
phase the subject was to push one of his buttons, after which his
"fellow-subject" was to push a button (actually the experimenter
administered what appeared to be the "fellow-subject's" responses). Thirty such interchanges were run in which the "fellow-
subject" administered either reinforcement (point) or punishment
(shock) equally often and on a random basis. None of the subject's
responses were differentially rewarded or punished during this
first phase of the experiment. During the second or conditioning
phase of the experiment, 80 trials were run in which the subject
was administered a shock at his pain-threshold level following
90% of the times he pushed either the "point" button or the
"shock" button. After 90% of the trials on which he administered
a shock to himself (at 3/4 of his pain-threshold intensity) he was
reinforced with a "point" from his "fellow-subject." In other
words, he soon could learn that administering a lesser self-shock
usually prevented a more severe shock from being administered to
him. In the third or extinction phase of the experiment, 30 trials
were run, with the "fellow-subject" returning to a random ad-
ministration of shocks and points; again, the subject's responses
were not differentially effective in avoiding shocks or earning
points.

A physiological measure of emotional arousal (vasoconstriction)
had been monitored throughout the experiment. During the sec-

ond (conditioning) phase of the experiment, self-shock responses became associated with faster physiological recovery times. In other words, self-shock responses became arousal-reducing. This is not surprising, since the subject learned that self-shock was usually followed by a reward, whereas shock or point responses were usually followed by an intense shock from the "fellow-subject." Also not surprising is the fact that during the conditioning phase the subjects increased the proportion of self-shock responses relative to the number of shock responses administered. During the third (extinction) phase the experimenters expected subjects to begin to use fewer self-shock responses, since they were no longer differentially effective. Unexpectedly, the proportion of self-shock responses relative to shock responses *increased* during the extinction period, even though such "self-punitive behavior" was no longer adaptive in terms of avoiding more severe punishments. These results can be interpreted in the light of our discussion of the power of fear and anxiety reduction as reinforcers. The self-shock response had been repeatedly reinforced by fear reduction and was therefore a persistent response, even though it was no longer adaptive.

There seems to be strong evidence that self-punitive or self-defeating behavior is established and maintained by the same principles of reinforcement and learning that establish and maintain other behaviors. In the case of self-defeating behaviors, the patterns of reinforcement are more complicated, but they seem generally to involve fear and anxiety reduction as reinforcers. Actually, the development of self-defeating behavior does not represent finding pleasure in pain as much as it represents behaving in a painful way to avoid a more painful alternative. In his behavioral analysis of "masochism," Brown (1965) cited the example of the religious fanatic who "may be viewed as one who finds pre-flagellation feelings of guilt and shame more 'painful' than the punishment itself."

So far, only the reinforcing effects of the reduction of painful emotions such as fear, anxiety, guilt, and shame have been mentioned. However, any reinforcer could maintain self-punitive behavior if its effects were powerful enough. Most people, for example, would willingly administer mild electric shocks to themselves at a thousand dollars a shot. In real life, however, few reinforcers are strong enough to induce the individual to inflict pain upon himself. One of the reinforcers that *is* strong enough is the reduction of greater pain, usually the pain of intense anxiety.

Conflict: external cues and internal cues

We can understand anxiety better if we make a somewhat arbitrary distinction between conflict over cues outside the individual and conflict over cues within the individual. This distinction is arbitrary because the individual must at least think about external-conflict cues, and thoughts are internal cues; however, the following discussion shows why a distinction is useful.

Externally cued conflict is represented by a study (Hovland & Sears, 1938) in which subjects were trained to draw a line toward a green light and away from a red light. After these responses had been well established, the subject was unexpectedly faced with the simultaneous presentation of red and green lights next to each other. Conditioned approach and avoidance responses to an object in the environment were thus elicited at the same time, resulting in inhibition or freezing responses in the subjects. At another level we might imagine a boy who develops strong affection for his cocker spaniel but who has a strong aversion to dachshunds as a result of being bitten by the neighbor's dachshund. If he should encounter a third dog bearing some resemblance to both a dachshund and a cocker spaniel (perhaps the result of his and the neighbor's dogs' indiscretions), the dog, because of stimulus generalization, will become an external cue for the boy's simultaneous approach and avoidance responses.

Externally cued conflicts should be differentiated from directly conditioned fears, which result from the experience of pain in the presence of some external cue. The boy, for example, is not in conflict over dachshunds (at least in theory); he has a directly conditioned fear of dachshunds.

Internally cued conflict (conflict over motivated impulses) and the principles by which such conflict develops are of considerably more importance to the understanding of neurosis. When an individual performs an overt response, he simultaneously performs internal responses such as thinking and feeling. If he is punished for his overt response, *committing that response becomes a cue for fear.* Since the concomitant thoughts and feelings were also present at the time of the punishment, they too can become fear-arousing cues; thinking particular thoughts can then become frightening. *If these thoughts and feelings are internally motivated,* they can become objects of approach-avoidance conflict, their occurrence being both desired and feared. That the punishment of thoughts and impulses can create *internalized (impulse-cued) conflict* is best illustrated by the example of the punishment of sexual behavior, especially among children. Nearly all children handle their own genitals at some time, and parents frequently respond by severely punishing this behavior. When they punish the overt behavior, the parents are also punishing the impulses and thoughts associated with that behavior. Thus, after an extensive series of experiences in which sexual behavior and the concomitant thoughts and impulses have been punished, the child's thoughts and impulses about sex acquire fear-inducing properties through conditioning. Since sexual behavior is innately motivated, an individual can become the victim of an internalized conflict in which his own unavoidable sexual thoughts and impulses are anxiety cues.

This principle of conflict development does not apply only to innately motivated behaviors, however. Most human behavior is based on secondary or learned drives, and it is entirely possible that learned drives can also be the basis of an internalized conflict. Feelings of dependency, especially among men, can bring about this sort of conflict, for example. Because of the conditions of early learning, nearly all humans develop dependency needs; nearly all humans need to be loved. In many situations, however, dependency needs are punished as unmanly. The individual can then develop an internalized conflict between a strongly learned drive and the punishing nature of the thoughts and impulses associated with that drive.

The devastating nature of internalized conflict stems primarily from the fact that there is no escape from such conflict. The cues emanate from within the person and are always present as long as the drives on which they are based are active. The most likely explanation of what has been called "free-floating anxiety," or nearly constant anxiety, is that such anxiety is either cued by many different things, so that the cues are never avoided, or cued by variables that are always present. It is obvious that the cues associated with internalized anxiety are always present for the individual with such a conflict. He is his own source of fear and anxiety.

It is important to remember that internalized conflict is seldom as simple as these examples suggest. In order to maintain an appropriate respect for the complexity of neurotic problems, we must recognize that an individual's conflicts are nearly always interrelated, multiple approach-avoidance conflicts of incredible complexity. Worell (1967) and others have demonstrated that conflicts tend to generalize so that one conflict intensifies other conflicts. In addition, it seems likely that anxious or neurotic individuals may develop conflicts with adverse effects on all their experience. For example, to the extent that stimulus hunger or exploratory needs are innately motivated, the punishments associated with new experiences conflict with those exploratory drives. The individual might be motivated to seek new experiences that result in his own growth but at the same time be afraid to do so (Butler & Rice, 1963).

Anxiety-avoiding behaviors ("symptoms")

With this brief description of how severe anxiety develops, we can move on to discuss the consequences of such severe anxiety. The individual in conflict is in a state of high drive, his condition is extremely aversive and motivating, and he has great need to resolve or avoid his conflict. In the literature on neurosis, the behaviors with which a person avoids conflict have traditionally been referred to as "symptoms." This practice is a carry-over from the treatment of neurotic problems as forms of medical problems; however, although the word "symptom" is a useful description of the observable effects of a physiological disorder, its use with neurotic problems has been somewhat misleading. It is more accurate to refer to neurotic "symptoms" as "anxiety-avoiding behaviors that are self-defeating," since they are the result of faulty learning experiences rather than the external signs of underlying forces in the same sense that medical symptoms are. Unfortunately, "symptom" is widely used in describing neurotic behavior, and no good substitute seems to have appeared yet. On occasion, therefore, the word "symptom" will be used in this discussion, but its use is based on the assumption that symptom means anxiety-avoiding behavior that is self-defeating.

The mechanism by which anxiety-avoiding behaviors develop is a complicated one in the life of any individual. The basic principle seems to be that, *through trial and error learning, some behaviors become effective in reducing anxiety and avoiding conflicts.* This means that any behavior that happens to be associated with anxiety reduction is strongly reinforced and therefore potentially a symptom. Some behaviors develop through reinforcement by anxiety-reduction but are *not* considered neurotic, primarily because they do not strike the individual and/or others as odd or strange, and they do not seem to bring long-term suffering. In fact, some of these behaviors are necessary for normal emotional adjustment. Two individuals with similar conflicts may learn different means of avoiding their conflicts; one set of behaviors may be socially acceptable and not lead to ultimate pain, while the other set may be clearly designated as neurotic by others and considered mal-adaptive in the self-punishing sense. All of us use some anxiety- and conflict-avoiding behaviors that are not defined as neurotic. However, as we move along the neurotic-normal continuum and our behaviors become more extreme, they will eventually be thought of as neurotic. The point at which a behavior is defined as neurotic is nearly impossible to establish, partly because there is no clear point at which a behavior becomes maladaptive or "odd"; society establishes different points at different times. An interesting example is society's view of smoking cigarettes. A few years ago smoking was widely accepted, but as evidence began to accumulate that smoking has a causal relationship to cancer and other diseases, the acceptability of smoking began to decrease. It is possible that some years from now smoking will be widely defined as a clearly neurotic behavior in the sense that it is ulti-mately harmful to the individual. People will see the immediate reward of smoking as being exchanged for an ultimate, much more severe punishment.

If *any* behavior can, under the right circumstances, function as an anxiety reducer and therefore potentially become a neurotic symptom, it may seem foolish to attempt to discuss specific symp-toms. As it happens, however, some patterns of anxiety-avoiding behaviors are quite common, primarily because of the inevitable similarities among learning histories of individuals in a culture. But as we discuss specific neurotic symptoms, keep in mind that the principles by which they develop are the same.

Phobias have received a great deal of attention and are widely misunderstood. A phobia has been defined as a morbid dread of an object or a fear disproportionate to the actual threat represented by an object. The term has been widely used recently with reference to *any* strong fear of a specific object. A useful distinction can be made, however, between "true" phobias and strong, directly conditioned fears. A phobia is a displaced fear that develops differently from directly conditioned fears. This distinction is important to understand and is probably best explained by the following case. A psychologist was called upon to treat a boy who was intensely afraid of dogs. Whenever a dog was in his neighborhood, the boy showed signs of strong fear and ran to hide under a chair. The psychologist quickly discovered that the boy had been badly bitten and scratched by a large dog, and his fear of dogs had clearly been directly conditioned by that experience. With this knowledge, the psychologist was then able to eliminate the fear of dogs through a counterconditioning procedure in which he gave the boy pleasant experiences, such as eating ice cream while watching a dog from a great distance. As pleasant experiences became associated with the sight of the dog, the animal was brought closer and the boy had greater contact with it.[2]

Compare this boy with another (hypothetical) boy with exactly the same symptoms. Our second boy has never had a painful experience in the presence of a dog; however, he does have a rather complicated conflictual problem. Because of his complicated learning experiences, the boy has strong dependency needs for his mother, but these needs have been severely punished. Thus, he has a complicated conflict in which he wants to approach his mother and be cuddled by her but is made fearful or anxious by these feelings and impulses. He wants to avoid his mother but can't stand to leave her, and he finds that any attempt to be dependent elicits from her a harsh admonition to leave the house

---

[2]This case is very similar to the classic one reported by Mary Cover Jones (1924). She modified "little Peter's" fear of rabbits through a similar counterconditioning procedure.

and play outside. The cues of his conflict are many and varied. He is in conflict about his own impulses. His mother is an approach-avoidance object outside of himself. He wants to leave the house to avoid his mother but can't stand to leave the house for fear of leaving his mother. However, if one day he happens to mention the presence of a large dog outside and his mother reacts by offering him some solace and telling him he doesn't have to go outside, his fearful act of avoiding the dog will be strongly reinforced as a partial resolution of his conflict, which happens to have followed his statement about the dog. He now has an "acceptable rationale" for staying with his mother, and some of his inner turmoil has been reduced. In other words, *fearing dogs has reduced his more severe anxiety.* Presumably, in the future this fear response will occur again, perhaps frequently and strongly; to the extent that it is conflict-reducing it will become a strong response. Although seemingly paradoxical, he will have developed *a fear that is anxiety-reducing.* His fear will be painful and will feel quite real to him; it will, however, be less painful than the conflict that it functions to avoid. It will thus be a displaced fear—a true phobia.

Any object can become a phobic object, depending on one's learning history. This is why many years ago psychologists gave up the attempt to establish lists of phobias such as "claustrophobia" and "agoraphobia." The lists quickly became cumbersome, for they are potentially endless.

I will briefly discuss a few other commonly mentioned symptoms, not so much to familiarize you with kinds of neurotic symptoms —most readers will already be familiar with common symptom patterns—as to illustrate the development of such symptoms in the light of the principles established so far. *Hysteria* (the development of physical symptoms with no physiological basis) is a classic neurotic symptom and was the basis of Freud's earliest work. Physical symptoms, although truly painful and debilitating, can develop through trial-and-error learning if the existence of these symptoms is anxiety-reducing. Obvious examples have occurred in wartime when physical symptoms such as paralysis have reduced the intolerable conflict of being forced to fight. At a less dramatic level, hysterical symptoms are often reinforced because of the effect they have on others' behavior. For example, the boy who developed a phobic fear of dogs might well, with a different learning history, have developed a physical symptom to serve the same reinforcing purposes. He might have fallen down the stairs and hurt his arm, receiving solace and being permitted to stay indoors. Then the existence of a hurt arm, rather than a fear of dogs, would be strongly reinforced. The pain response itself would persist.

Another classic symptom is *obsessive-compulsive* behavior, wherein the individual is unable to rid himself of a particular thought or unable to prevent himself from performing a particular act. The obsession and the compulsion can be very reinforcing, since they consume so much of the individual's thought and time that they permit him to avoid the thoughts and impulses and acts that are the basis of some other strong conflict.

Psychopathic behavior presents a complicated problem. Psychopathy is usually marked by impulsive, need-gratifying behavior, without concern for later consequences or the welfare of others. Some of this "acting out" seems to result from insufficient conscience training—too little anxiety. In some cases, however, such behavior seems to serve a neurotic, anxiety-reducing function. It is conceivable that an anxious person might avoid the elements of his real conflicts by continuously being "in trouble." In this case, his "acting out" behavior would be a neurotic symptom in the sense that it is self-defeating but maintained by anxiety reduction. For example, a man might repeatedly seduce and then hurt women. His behavior might be described as "psychopathic" or "acting out," but its causes either could be the result of insufficiently developed feelings of conscience ("too little anxiety") or could reflect some intense conflict. He might, for example, desperately want intimacy and love but desperately fear it at the same time; his behavior would be an anxiety-reducing "symptom" and its treatment would involve treating his anxiety. In the former case, though, the same behavior would not be a symptom in the sense that it is anxiety reducing, and treatment aimed at lowering anxiety even further might result in even more of the destructive behavior.

What have classically been called *defense mechanisms* also fit the definition of "symptoms" when they cause self-defeating behavior. Projection, rationalization, reaction formation, and denial, for example, can all be used as anxiety-reducing behaviors, which are defined as neurotic or as defensive only when they involve the distortion of reality as it appears to other people or when they result in self-defeating behavior. These behaviors have no special status; they happen to be behaviors that often work as anxiety-reducers. In a sense, the list of defense mechanisms is as potentially endless as the list of phobias. All individuals use defense mechanisms and within limits they are adaptive and necessary for our survival. We again must keep in mind that neurotic behavior and normal behavior are not different qualitatively; they differ only along continua. Any individual who uses defensive (that is, reality distorting) mechanisms is to some extent "neurotic" but is not defined as such until his use of these mechanisms becomes so extreme that it is intolerable to himself and/or to others.

Repression and unconscious influences on behavior. *Repression* is usually mentioned as one of the defense mechanisms, but I think it deserves special attention because it underlies the way people lie to themselves and thus underlies both all defense mechanisms and unconscious influences on behavior. (Freud formulated it as the most important of the defenses.) Repression is the unintentional forgetting of stimuli that have been learned sufficiently strongly to be remembered under normal circumstances. Normal forgetting, in contrast, is the result of insufficient reinforcement of the stimuli involved—the result of insufficient learning or of interference from other learning. Repression should also be contrasted with suppression, which is the conscious (verbally mediated) stopping of a particular thought—the decision "let's not think about things like that anymore." Since repression is *unintentional* forgetting, a person obviously cannot decide to repress something; the process is automatic. Probably the most useful theoretical treatment of how repression works is still that of Dollard and Miller (1950). (See also Shaffer & Shoben, 1956.) The process is basically that of *inhibiting the response of thinking particular thoughts.* To understand this formulation it is necessary to realize that thoughts are not *things;* they are responses. If thinking a particular thought—that is, performing a particular response—leads to punishment (as it does with a painful thought), the individual will be less likely to perform that response—to think that thought in the future. If the particular brain processes associated with a painful thought lead to punishment, those particular brain processes will be less likely to occur in the future. With repetition of such experiences, the thinking of a particular thought will become inhibited—that is, it will not occur. The process of inhibition is more easily understood in relation to responses other than thinking. If a child, for example, is severely and repeatedly punished for kicking his parents, the kicking response will eventually stop occurring; the action and the thoughts (verbal responses) associated with it will be inhibited. The potential for the kicking response exists in the structure of the leg and the nerves of the child, just as the thought potential is in the structure of the brain. However, when the thought is repressed, it does not go anywhere like an "unconscious mind"; it simply does not occur. It is through this process that unintentional —that is, not verbally mediated—forgetting can occur.

In one experiment on repression (Ericksen & Kuethe, 1956), subjects were presented with 15 stimulus words and were instructed to say the first word that came to mind in association with the stimulus word. On five of the word associations (randomly chosen), the subject received a painful shock. Subsequently, the list of stimulus words was repeated as many as 10 times and subjects were given shock only when they repeated the particular word association that had been shocked in the first trial. It was thus possible for subjects to avoid further shocks by giving a new word association to the five stimulus words that had been shocked originally. The subjects had been told that they would be shocked for going too slowly or for some other undisclosed reason that they might discover. In the second phase of the experiment subjects were asked to give as many word associations to the stimulus words as they could and were given 15 seconds per word to give these associations. During this phase subjects were informed that no more shocks would be given. At the end of the experiment the experimenters interviewed each subject in order to discover which ones could verbalize the method of avoiding shocks. They were able to classify their subjects into three groups: an "insight group," 11 subjects who had figured out how to avoid the shocks and could verbalize their reasons; the "no-insight group," 11 subjects who could verbalize no systematic reason for the shocks; and a third unclassifiable group of 5 subjects who had arrived at a system that worked but that was incorrect in terms of the design of the experiment (for example, one subject began saying "good or bad" for all of his associations, thus successfully avoiding his initial association). Figure 3–7 presents Ericksen and Kuethe's results, and it is obvious that the "insight group" continued to repeat their initial associations to the safe words and eventually eliminated repetitions of their initial associations to the shocked words. This was certainly to be expected, since they had figured out the cause of the shocks. Of interest to our discussion of repression are the results of the "no-insight group." They also continued their initial associations to the safe words at a high rate of repetitions but showed a clear decline in their repetitions of the initial associations to the shocked words. A possible criticism of Ericksen and Kuethe's finding is that the "no-insight group" may really have figured out how to avoid shock and for some reason had not told the experimenter about it. To check on this possibility Ericksen and Kuethe analyzed the reaction times required for each word association. In Figure 3–8 the reaction times for the shocked and

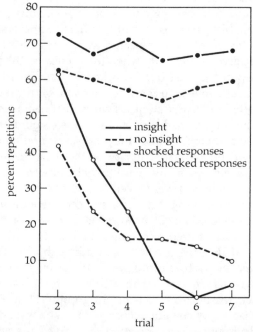

Figure 3–7. Percentage of first-trial responses repeated on succeeding trials as a function of punishment. (From Eriksen & Kuethe, 1956. Copyright by the American Psychological Association and reproduced with permission.)

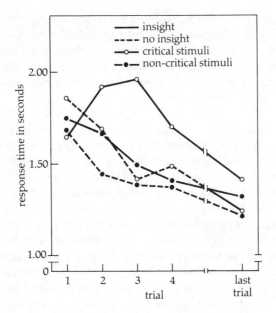

Figure 3–8. Reaction times to critical and non-critical stimuli as a function of trials. (Eriksen & Kuethe, 1956. Copyright by the American Psychological Association and reprinted by permisssion.)

safe words are presented for the insight group, and it is obvious that there was an initial sharp increase in reaction time on the shocked words. These subjects apparently responded more quickly to the safe words but required more time on the shocked words, presumably to suppress their initial association and to find an alternative. Once they had found a safe association to the previously shocked words, the reaction time on the shocked words also decreased. Also in Figure 3–8 are the reaction times for the "no-insight group." Their reactions to the shocked and safe words did not take differentially greater times, and they did not appear to go through the same process of searching for an alternative word that the insight group had gone through on the shocked words. It seems reasonable to draw analogies between the process the "insight group" used and *suppression* and between the process the "no-insight group" used and *repression*. The "no-insight group" seemed to inhibit thinking the previously shocked words automatically, without knowing why. Further support for this formulation is found in the results reported for the second phase of the experiment, when subjects gave chained associations to the stimulus words. Here again, for both groups of subjects more safe words were produced than were shocked words, even though the shock had been completely discontinued and even though the initial shocked associations were obviously strong responses in each subject's response hierarchy.

All individuals repress, because repression is necessary for survival; it is one of the most effective ways to avoid the elements of an internally cued conflict. Whether or not repression has consequences that will eventually be labeled as neurotic depends on a number of factors. Repression leaves the individual with incomplete knowledge, since some of his memories are no longer available to him. If a situation arises where that particular knowledge is necessary for adaptive behavior, he obviously will be hurt by his repression. More importantly, perhaps, repression is not total; an impulse or thought that has been inhibited can occur in a poorly verbalized form—that is, be partially repressed—and still arouse anxiety. Strong environmental stimuli may make repression difficult to maintain, such as when the individual is faced with strong external evidence that some repressed event actually occurred. In addition, the thoughts and impulses that have been repressed can be so strongly motivated internally that the inhibition or repression process simply cannot prevent their occurrence, at least in partial form. This is illustrated, for example, by the repression of sexual thoughts and impulses which, especially in adolescence, are so strongly motivated that repression is often an ineffective anxiety-avoiding behavior. Feared thoughts can occur in poorly verbalized form, serving to cue fear responses whose causes the individual can't understand.

Our understanding of *unconscious influences on behavior* is built on our understanding of partial repression. Conscious thoughts consist of brain processes that can be verbalized (or, more precisely, symbolized). Thoughts are responses and can occur partially, just as any other response can occur in partial form. To the extent that brain processes are "verbalizable," they are conscious thoughts. Brain processes can be partially verbalizable—perhaps because of a lack of verbal labels, perhaps because of partial repression of relevant brain processes. Partially verbalizable brain processes are partially conscious, an observation that points out that "conscious" and "unconscious" are on a continuum, and it is inaccurate to speak of thoughts as *either* conscious or unconscious. By now, I hope it is clear why it is inaccurate to say things like "In his unconscious mind he hates his father, so his unconscious mind made him punish his father by failing in his father's business." Partially conscious thoughts and concomitant feelings *do* affect behavior, and we might have said that this hypothetical client has poorly verbalized feelings as well as thoughts of hatred that are so unacceptable they have been partially repressed. In their partially repressed form they can still serve as fear cues, and whatever the young man does that leads to fear reduction will be strongly reinforced, even though he may not be able to understand (verbalize) what is going on. He might say, "I can't understand why I do these dumb things. I want to make a success of my own life and I love my father so much I want the business to succeed for his sake too." He is responding to his partially conscious hatred, just as we all act in accordance with partially verbalized motives at times. When an intense conflict is partially repressed, anything that helps relieve the conflict is very strongly reinforced—even self-destructive behavior. Our young man has an internalized conflict in which his aggressive feelings are strongly motivated but are also strongly fear arousing. If his feelings didn't frighten him so much he could think about them more accurately and engage in more adaptive problem solving.

Anxiety states

The previous sections have implied that an individual in a state of conflict develops anxiety-avoiding behaviors that may be neurotic but do help him avoid anxiety. This is not always the case, because individuals are often in a state of unavoidable conflict, in which they suffer without relief. It may be that no anxiety-avoiding behavior is available; it may be that the elements of the conflict are so strong that avoidance behaviors are ineffective (as can be the case with the repression of sexual thoughts and impulses); or it may be that a potentially "successful" avoidance behavior is available but the individual has had no experience with it. In any case, the person may be suffering from what has been called an anxiety-state neurosis. He experiences frequent anxiety attacks, which can only be seen as suffering responses. What we call neurotic anxiety is not necessarily functional in the same way that phobic fears, for

example, are functional in anxiety reduction. Anxiety-state neuroses are, in a sense, "unsuccessful neuroses"; symptoms have not
developed or have become insufficient.

Anxiety states can be marked by a haunting, helpless, near panic
which ebbs and flows, sometimes reaching an unbearable level
where nothing seems to bring relief. For each individual the anxiety means something different. It might be identified as guilt,
depression, anxiety, fear, or some other painful emotion. The victim doesn't know why he is anxious. When he tries to understand,
he grasps nothing. A theoretical explanation of these feelings
seems dry and unreal next to the intensity of the feeling, but, in
general, anxiety states result from intense internalized conflicts
whose cues are only partially repressed. The partial repression
permits the feared impulses and thoughts to elicit anxiety, but
because the cues are not verbalized (or are not even capable of
being verbalized) relearning of the responses to feared cues is
prevented. We will see that one task of therapy is to lessen repression and other ways of avoiding anxiety cues and to permit relearning of responses to those cues.

In the practice of psychotherapy it is often the person who is in
a state of anxiety who appears for help, since he is the one who
is most strongly motivated to seek help. He has been unsuccessful
at reducing his own anxiety and he seeks psychotherapy as a
potential anxiety reducer. If, on the other hand, his symptoms are
"working" for him and don't bother other people he may have no
motivation to seek psychotherapy (it may even be inappropriate
to call such anxiety-avoiding behaviors "symptoms," since they
are defined by the individual and by those around him as acceptable or adaptive).

One of the most frequently observed characteristics of persons
suffering from anxiety is that of a self-deprecating feeling of
worthlessness—a feeling that somehow he is an intrinsically bad
or unworthy person. This experience is probably a consequence of
internally cued conflict. What each of us refers to as "me" or "I"
or "myself" is the sum total of what our thoughts and feelings and
impulses and acts are. If those thoughts, impulses, and acts cue
anxiety responses, the individual is his own source of anxiety—
what he *is* makes him anxious. What he *is* feels bad and unaccept-

able. It is probably in this light that Rogers' notion of "conditions of worth" can best be understood. "Conditions of worth" develop when significant others give a child positive regard only on the condition that he not have certain feelings or experiences. The individual then comes to value himself conditionally—only if he does not have the "bad" characteristics. When these characteristics are a part of experience, they must be denied or distorted. He is, in other words, the victim of an internalized conflict that makes him feel unworthy. As Shaffer and Shoben (1956) have said, "Anxiety is sensed as personal and pervasive. It arises from a conflict of one's own impulses and is ascribed to oneself" (p. 121).

The inability to learn

The vicious circle in which neurotic behavior traps individuals is due to the fact that the neurotic behavior serves to avoid the conflict cues and prevent relearning associated with the conflict. The anxiety will not evaporate or disappear on its own. The responses to the elements of the conflict must be relearned or reconditioned.[3] An instructive principle can be drawn from Brown's "masochistic" rats who ran out of the no-longer-electrified start box so fast that there was no time to relearn new responses to the surrounding cues. The fear-inducing cues were avoided before relearning could occur. A similar fear-avoiding process causes the neurotic person to distort cues and to hold on to inadequate information, all in the service of anxiety reduction but at the cost of ultimate suffering. There is considerable evidence (Easterbrook, 1959; Zaffy & Bruning, 1966; Bruning et al., 1968) that anxiety causes the individual to use fewer of the cues available to him for problem-solving. In addition, high anxiety states lead to a decreased ability to discriminate between stimuli that could be discriminated by the individual prior to his conflict or that other nonanxious subjects could discriminate. Anxiety constricts behavior. If exploration in the past has been painful, anxiety will reduce the individual's tendency to explore both his environment and his own feelings and impulses. His reduced self-exploration in turn prevents finding new solutions, and he is unable to learn because the process is too painful.

[3]It could also be argued that these responses can be extinguished, but in such cases extinction can probably be most accurately thought of as a form of counterconditioning (see Chapter 4).

A clear distinction must be made between the inability to learn and the lack of opportunity to learn. The problems we are discussing as neurotic are related to the inability to learn, even when the cues for new learning are available. Some individuals, it seems reasonable to say, behave in a maladaptive or apparently neurotic way simply because they have never been taught any differently; they have not been exposed to the experiences necessary to learn a more adaptive way to behave, or they have only neurotic models to imitate (Bandura, 1969). As I will show in my model of psychotherapy, this is an important distinction to make, since simply teaching a neurotic person may be totally ineffective if he is unable to learn. If the problem, however, is that he simply has lacked the opportunity to learn, direct teaching might be quite appropriate. Further, if he is unable to learn at the beginning of psychotherapy, relief of his conflicts may enable him to learn later, but he may lack the opportunities; that situation can become an appropriate one for direct teaching.

This brief review of the nature of neurotic conflict and its consequences has established the following picture of the individual suffering from anxiety-based neurotic problems: to the extent that anxiety is an important problem, the individual is caught in a number of complicated *conflicts*. As a result of his conflicts the potential client comes to therapy sometimes with *"symptoms"*; often he is suffering from *anxiety* whose cues he only partly understands; and he usually comes with an *impaired ability to solve his own problems,* usually in the interpersonal area, and almost always because he is avoiding relevant cues that he otherwise would be using in his problem-solving attempts. Finally, the potential client often feels *low self-esteem* and a painful distaste for what he is.

4

Relieving conflicts — in theory

The therapist's task is to help his client lessen the intensity of conflicts (none of us is ever entirely free of conflicts) and thus to free him from his excessive anxiety, to relieve the need for his symptoms, to help him establish more effective problem-solving approaches to life, and to help him achieve greater acceptance of himself. Broadly stated, these are the goals of therapy. They will be discussed in more detail in Chapter 6 and at that time some of the difficult issues involved in establishing a definition of emotional health will be considered. This chapter develops a theoretical model to explain the central processes of psychotherapy, and the following chapters translate the theoretical model into practice.

The task of therapists is a very complex one, and there are several dangers in attempting to reduce the processes of psychotherapy to writing. One danger especially in this chapter is that of sounding detached, mechanical, and simplistic. My goal in developing a theoretical model is to provide as simplified a description of the essential factors of psychotherapy as possible, while still integrating all of the important variables in the process. The job here is to spell out the principles. I will later apply these principles to the more complex situations of actual psychotherapy.

A second danger is that in describing the *central* processes by which psychotherapy works I may give the impression that the therapist's behavior can always be fitted into a few categories. Many behaviors are required of psychotherapists which do not readily apply to the process to be described as the central therapeutic process. Some of the complexity of the therapist's task is communicated in Chapter 7, which discusses special problems that do not readily fit into my theoretical model.

Relieving conflicts

The theoretical model I will use to discuss therapy in the rest of the book is based on the principles of conflict resolution. You will recognize Figure 4-1 as Miller's diagram of the simple approach-avoidance conflict discussed in Chapter 3. Nearly all human conflicts and human problems involve extremely complicated, intertwined multiple approach-avoidance conflicts and should be understood in those terms. For the sake of explanation, however, Miller's diagram can be used to examine some of the dynamics of conflict and of the relief of conflicts. Recall that one of the characteristics of conflict is that the strength of the approach and avoid-

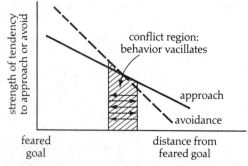

Figure 4–1. Diagram of approach-avoidance conflict showing the conflict area, in which behavior will vacillate between approach and avoidance.

ance tendencies varies according to the strength of the drives on which the tendencies are based. Relieving an approach-avoidance conflict would involve either (or both) strengthening the overall approach tendency (raising the approach gradient) or weakening the avoidance tendency (lowering the avoidance gradient). There are probably some instances in which the therapist can increase a client's approach tendencies for the elements of his conflicts, but in the therapy situation it is more within the therapist's ability to lower the avoidance gradient—that is, to weaken the fear responses associated with the cues that are important to the individual.

Another important characteristic of the approach-avoidance conflict is that the point at which the gradients cross is presumably the point at which approach behavior will stop. This area, however, is more accurately thought of as a region in which behavior vacillates and not a point at which behavior stops (Brown, 1948; Miller, 1944; Phillips, 1956). The individual is engaged in a continuous process of approach and retreat. Because of his tendency to approach the feared goal he will get as close as he can to the elements of his conflict, but as soon as his avoidance responses (anxieties) become predominant he will retreat (thus avoiding the anxiety-arousing cues) to a point where he again has a strong enough approach tendency to motivate an approach to the cues—an approach that will again result in a retreat.

The conflicted individual is in a conflict region and not at a conflict point. He will get as close to a full realization of the elements of his conflict as he can stand to get and then will retreat. To state it loosely, the conflicted individual will look at as much of the "truth" about himself as he can stand to look at and then will stop looking. The therapist's task is to lessen the client's fear of his own impulses and thoughts and to facilitate the client's fuller realization of the elements of his conflicts, enabling the client to figure out more adaptive ways to behave.

Relieving a conflict by lowering the avoidance gradient requires that two things be done. First the individual must be *held in the presence of the anxiety-arousing cues* so that relearning can be associated with these cues. Without such intervention the individual retreats so quickly from the anxiety-arousing cues that there is no chance for relearning to take place. At the same time that the individual is being held in the presence of the anxiety-arousing cues it is necessary that these cues be counterconditioned by being paired with some pleasant stimulus, some *counterconditioning agent.* It can be argued that simply holding the individual in the presence of the anxiety-provoking cues would be sufficient, since his anxiety response would extinguish in the absence of punishment. Such an instance, however, can probably be best understood as one form of counterconditioning, since the person is being exposed to the cues, certainly in the absence of punishment, but also in the *presence* of many other influences such as a comfortable temperature, a pleasantly decorated room, an expert therapist, and any of countless other pleasant stimuli. Extinction in this case seems to be a form of counterconditioning, since it is absurd to think of holding the individual in the presence of anxiety-provoking cues in the absence of everything else. If the cues are paired with unpleasant stimuli, the anxiety or fear responses are strengthened. If they are paired with pleasant stimuli, the fear responses are weakened. In any case, the fear response is weakened more rapidly when a specific attempt is made to pair the fear cues with a pleasant stimulus than when the nature of the counterconditioning agent is not specified and "extinction" presumably is taking place (see Bandura, 1969, Chapter 8).

Working in the conflict region

The principles of conflict relief can now be applied to the psychotherapy client's situation in a way to maximally achieve the goals of therapy as outlined at the beginning of this chapter. The therapist's task, in theoretical terms, is to hold the client in the presence of his anxiety cues and provide a counterconditioning agent at the same time. It is important, for reasons to be discussed in detail later, that the therapist intervene at the point of *the client's greatest approach* to the elements of his own conflict. In theoretical terms the therapist must intervene at the *leading edge of the conflict region.* The leading edge of the conflict region consists of material the client is trying to communicate but hasn't quite verbalized—content and feeling that are *implicit in the message the client is intending to communicate.* (I will elaborate on how the therapist perceives "the leading edge of the conflict region" in the next chapter.) When the client attempts to deal with anxiety-provoking material, the therapist responds to the anxiety-provoking cues, thus "holding the client in the presence of those cues." The therapist prevents the vacillation within the conflict region by verbalizing the cues associated with the leading edge of the conflict region. At the same time, he provides some kind of counterconditioning agent, which I will argue can most effectively be thought of as what is usually called a "good relationship." What is meant by a "good relationship" will be discussed later, but for now assume that the therapist can provide a counterconditioning agent, a pleasant stimulus to be paired with the mildly anxiety-provoking cues associated with the leading edge of the conflict region.

The key issue. The crucial difference between this attempt to understand therapy in terms of learning and the attempts of Dollard and Miller, Shoben, and other more directive therapists is this: *the therapist responds to the client's approach response.* It is the client in this sense who determines the course of therapy by attempting to approach the elements of his conflict. It is not the therapist's job to point out the elements of the conflict or to be the client's teacher. It is the therapist's job to hear the client attempt to approach the elements of his own conflict—to explore himself. And it is at this point that the therapist intervenes. This is a central issue, since Rogers' position is that in client-centered therapy the client has primary responsibility for determining the course of therapy, and the therapist's job is to facilitate the growth process by providing empathy, warmth, and congruence. I am saying more specifically that the central therapeutic process occurs when the therapist responds to the client's approach responses. Rogers has said that his approach works because the client has an innate self-actualizing tendency, but I and others have challenged theoretical positions based on self-actualizing tendencies. By understanding neurosis as the result of conflict, a therapist can base his faith that the client can direct the course of therapy (with the therapist's help) on the nature of conflict. *The client will approach the elements of his conflict.* If a conflict exists, the client has an approach tendency that will lead him to come "as close to the truth" as he can stand to come, and he will do so repeatedly. The therapist's job is to help him not to retreat from the elements of his conflicts. If there is no approach tendency there is no conflict, and in such a case behavior modification might be appropriate (see Chapter 9).

The nature of conflict has established the basis for our trust in the client's capacity to solve his own problems, with a specific kind of help from the therapist. This theoretical model need depend only on this formulation of the nature of conflict. It is further enhanced, however, if stimulus hunger is a primary source of drive, a possibility we discussed in Chapters 1 and 2. Butler and Rice (1963) have argued that stimulus hunger results in a need for new experiences. They have proposed that this tendency to seek new experiences provides a basis for the position that clients have the capacity to seek out new solutions for themselves, providing a possible reinterpretation of Rogers' thinking on self-actualizing tendencies. In my terms, the individual will attempt to approach the elements of his own conflict. Because of the nature of conflict and possibly because of his tendency to seek new experience, a tendency that has been blocked by the anxiety associated with new experience, the client can be depended on to "direct" the course of therapy.

Step-by-step progress. If in the therapy process the therapist has successfully responded to the anxiety-provoking cues that the client has approached, and if counterconditioning takes place, the result will be a weakening of the avoidance response—that is, a lowering of the avoidance gradient, as illustrated in Figure 4–2. The result of lowering the avoidance gradient is that the conflict region moves closer toward the feared goal. That is, the point at which behavior will begin to vacillate is now closer to the elements of the conflict being avoided. The cues that previously were anxi-

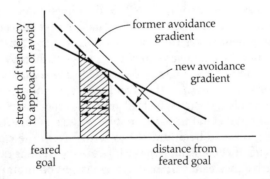

Figure 4–2. Weakening the strength of avoidance moves the conflict region closer to the feared goal.

ety-arousing now are neutral or at least are less anxiety-arousing than the client's approach response at the previous intersection point. By enabling the client to approach the elements of his conflict to a slight extent, the therapist has set the stage to enable him to take a further step. Assuming that his avoidance tendency has been weakened, material that was previously too painful to look at can now be handled comfortably, and it becomes possible to deal with further aspects of the conflict. The therapist enables the client to approach the "truth" about the elements of his conflict in a step-by-step progression.

Reinforcing the client's approach responses. In addition to the process of counterconditioning previously feared cues, a second and extremely important therapeutic benefit results from the therapist's responding specifically to the client's attempt at approaching the elements of his conflicts. You will recall that the therapist's task is not to force the client into the presence of the anxiety cues. He waits until the client initiates an approach to anxiety-provoking cues, and he responds at that point. Not only, then, is counterconditioning associated with the cues but *the client is strongly reinforced for his approach response*—that is, for his attempt at self-exploration. If the therapist responds effectively, each of the client's approach responses will be followed by anxiety reduction, and the client's problem-solving attempts will be repeatedly reinforced by increments of anxiety reduction. There are undoubtedly also other reinforcing agents of a social nature that are not directly related to the process of anxiety reduction. For example, differentially provided attention from the therapist, at the time self-exploration takes place, probably also serves to reinforce self-exploration.

The step-by-step approach to the full realization of the elements of the conflict results in the client's continuing new awareness of cues that were previously too painful to be dealt with. Human conflicts, especially those faced by people with neurotic problems, are incredibly complex. As counterconditioning takes place in a step-by-step progression, new cues become available, and one consequence of this is that both therapist's and client's earlier understandings of the nature of the problem will almost always prove to be inaccurate, since they were based on incomplete knowledge of the cues involved. To borrow a behavior-modification term, the client is progressing through an "anxiety hierarchy" as he moves to more and more anxiety-provoking cues, and the nature of the hierarchy continually changes as more and more cues become available to increase his understanding. A consequence of this is that an anxiety-hierarchy established at any point in therapy will necessarily be at least partially incorrect. The process of therapy I am describing permits the therapist and client to modify continuously the nature of the hierarchy, as correction of it becomes necessary with new knowledge. Clients do indeed progress in therapy along an anxiety hierarchy, but it is a hierarchy that the client and therapist discover together during the therapy process. The client will attempt to take the next step on his hierarchy. The therapist's job is to hear this attempt and to facilitate it by responding to the leading edge of what the client is trying to deal with. (See below and Chapter 8 for more comparisons with behavior modification.)

The role of "insight." The concept of "insight" has occupied much attention in writing about psychotherapy, even though it has proved very difficult to define and understand. Generally, the word has been used to describe the process of seeing new knowledge or gaining new understanding in a relatively sudden way and with relatively strong emotion. Probably because of their dramatic nature and their obvious importance to clients, moments of insight have attracted attention disproportionate to their frequency in psychotherapy. It has seemed to many writers that the experience of insight is associated with moments of therapeutic growth, and many have, on this basis, argued that insight *causes* therapeutic growth. They have therefore tried to provide their clients with directly given new knowledge as a therapeutic technique. Nearly all therapists, however, have recognized the difficult-to-deal-with fact that in most cases knowledge alone does not bring insight. The conflict model suggests that insight is not a cause of therapeutic growth but rather an effect. An emotional release occasionally accompanies the sudden realization of a new understanding as counterconditioning (anxiety reduction) takes place—that is, as previously painful cues become less painful. Knowledge and information are important components of the psychotherapy process; but it is not the knowledge alone that makes the client free, it is the process by which he acquires the knowledge. He benefits most when self-exploration is accompanied by counterconditioning.

Leading or following?   Many writers in the field of psychotherapy have characterized Rogers' approach as that of following the client and the more directive approaches, such as those of Dollard and Miller, Ellis, and others, as that of leading the client. This distinction is almost always overstated, and in the light of the present model the question "should the therapist lead or follow?" cannot be meaningfully answered, since he is doing both. He is following the client in the sense that he listens intently for the direction the client is trying to take, but he then responds to the client's exploratory attempts in a way that can be described as leading. He does not repeat back what the client has said. He responds to the painful edge of what the client is *trying to say.*

The function of the relationship.   The most powerful counterconditioning agent in psychotherapy is the relationship. It is difficult to define a "good relationship" in theoretical terms and even more difficult to translate that definition into behavioral terms. In general, relationship can be defined as a collective term for those behaviors that mutually affect two or more people. Some theorists have given "relationship" the status of an entity or a force with a somewhat mystical aura about it (Dreyfus, 1962). To avoid slipping into that kind of language, I will say that a relationship as a counterconditioning agent can be defined as behaviors that are provided by the therapist, that have an effect on the client, and that provide, in some way, a rewarding or pleasant situation. For a relationship to act as a counterconditioning agent—that is, to be a "good relationship"—the therapist must certainly be nonpunishing; he must somehow also provide rewarding social behaviors. Whether these behaviors can be described as permissiveness, nonpossessive warmth, acceptance, congruence, respect, prizing, or something else will be discussed in detail in the next chapter. It may be that such qualities do provide a rewarding or pleasant situation for the client, and if that is the case they can function as counterconditioning agents. The difficulty is that for some individuals "warm" behavior has been associated in the past with punishment, as in the case of a person whose parents' "warm" and "loving" behavior was accompanied by subtle and overt painful punishment or by inconsistent rejection. No particular therapist behavior is inherently a counterconditioner. It may be that for most individuals a particular behavior (such as warmth) may provide a rewarding social atmosphere, but it is the therapist's job to provide for each individual client an atmosphere that is not only nonpunitive but also in some way socially rewarding.

An interesting consequence of this analysis is that "relationship" could conceivably involve all characteristics of the therapy situation. If, for example, the therapist's office were painted a depressing black, the therapy situation might be less effective as a counterconditioning agent. Less facetiously, the counterconditioning capacity of the therapeutic situation is evidently affected by such things as the client's expectations about the therapist, the therapist's reputation, his physical appearance, and other factors that cannot easily be incorporated within the concept "relationship" (Grosz, 1968; Parsons & Parker, 1968; Carkhuff & Pierce, 1967).

Comparisons with other counterconditioning agents

It is probably too glib to call the therapeutic relationship *the* effective counterconditioning agent in psychotherapy. The question can legitimately be asked whether there might be equally or more effective counterconditioning agents available. Shoben (1949) dealt with this issue in making a very similar argument that the relationship is a counterconditioning agent. An acquaintance of Shoben's had asked him why a warm bath might not also function as a counterconditioning agent. Shoben's answer (which I would agree with) was that the fears and anxieties of neurosis involve strong social punishment, and to be useful a counterconditioning agent must be equally strong and, in order to be sufficiently strong, may have to be social in nature. In addition, if the process of psychotherapy involves pairing the client's approach to previously anxiety-provoking cues with the counterconditioning agent, it might be difficult to apply a tub of warm water specifically at the time of such self-exploratory responses. To be effective, a counterconditioning agent not only must be strong but must be specifically applicable at the moment the client attempts an approach response. Theoretically any counterconditioning agent that meets these two criteria would be appropriate for the present model. However, it seems most likely that the behaviors associated with "good relationships" most adequately meet the criteria of being strongly reinforcing (and of a social nature) and being precisely applicable at the moment the client attempts an approach response to the elements of his conflict. At such moments the therapist communicates his interest and understanding, both verbally and nonverbally.

Bandura (1969) has argued that, although relationship-induced responses can serve to countercondition emotional arousal, they have a number of disadvantages. He cites the discouraging outcome data reported for relationship-oriented approaches, but here he has lumped together all interview therapy and ignored the considerable evidence specifically for the efficacy of empathy and warmth behaviors. He also says that "Relationship-produced responses cannot be easily controlled or rapidly increased if necessary" (p. 483). This is only partially true, since the therapist does have considerable control over the timing of the communication of behaviors that constitute a relationship. More significantly, these social behaviors are, more than other counterconditioning agents, reliably applicable in response to *client-initiated* approach responses. Bandura's third argument is that the effects of counterconditioning "would remain unpredictable if the introduction of emotionally disturbing contents was primarily left to the vagaries of clients, rather than carefully regulated by psychotherapists" (p. 484). My response is that, because of the nature of conflict, the client's "vagaries" are not vagaries at all. The course of counterconditioning is most accurately and usefully directed by the client's approach responses. A psychotherapist's "careful regulation" might indeed make therapy more *predictable,* but the most accurate and effective identification of the relevant stimulus determinants requires a continuously modified exploration process.

An obvious comparison can be drawn between my conception of the relationship as a counterconditioning agent and Wolpe's use of relaxation as a counterconditioning agent. The principles and many of the phrases I use, such as "anxiety hierarchy,"are similar to Wolpe's. However, it is obvious that my application of the principles differs considerably from that proposed by Wolpe. The differences lie primarily in the choice of a counterconditioning agent, in the means of making it available to the client, and in the specification of disorders for which different techniques are appropriate. Wolpe's techniques do seem to have useful applications that will be discussed in a later chapter. But for dealing with internalized conflicts relaxation is probably not a strong socially-based counterconditioning agent, and in any case, relaxation would be difficult to "apply" at the moment when a client makes a self-exploratory attempt (an approach response to the elements of his conflict).

I have theorized in this chapter that the central therapeutic process involves two major elements: (1) the therapist's response to the leading edge of the client's self-exploratory attempts and (2) his ensuring that this process take place in the environment best described as a "good relationship." One implication of this formulation is that the first element alone is insufficient for therapeutic growth and may have unfortunate consequences. The therapist's response to the anxiety-provoking cues that the client approaches will not be anxiety-reducing or reinforcing of the approach response unless a counterconditioning agent is present. The therapist's "leadingly empathic" response (as I shall loosely call it for now) would hold the client in the presence of the anxiety-provoking cues but would not countercondition the anxiety associated with the cues and would be experienced by the client as an anxiety-arousing event. The therapy situation must have some counterconditioning power before the anxiety-arousing cues can be dealt with. Stated more loosely but perhaps more understandably, a good relationship must be built before painful self-exploration can be therapeutic. It seems likely that in the early stages of therapy the client is learning whether the therapist can be trusted emotionally—that is, whether the therapist will engage in the socially attacking behavior that the client may have experienced elsewhere. The therapist's job in the early stages of therapy is to be attentive and accepting and to begin the long process of reinforcing the client's attempts at self-exploration—not necessarily, as is the case later, with leadingly empathic responses but with warm attentiveness and nonanxiety-arousing understanding. Being "too deeply empathic" early in therapy can result in premature termination (Truax & Carkhuff, 1963).

Before leaving this theoretical chapter I want to repeat the warning at the beginning of the chapter about the danger of oversimplification. Remember that we have been discussing the *central* therapeutic processes. No attempt has been made to reduce everything that a therapist does to one or two principles. It is likely, for example, that responding only to mildly anxiety-provoking material would weaken the therapist's status as a counterconditioning agent and that much effort may necessarily be devoted to building the relationship or simply to responding to the act of self-exploration in nonthreatening areas. It must be remembered that many other therapist behaviors may be necessary prior to the client's being able to take therapeutic steps.

5

Relieving conflicts — in practice

The previous chapter provided a relatively formal and perhaps sterile account of the therapy process. To translate my theoretical model into the practice of therapy I will need to use more informal and loosely constructed descriptions of behavior; I will also frequently refer to the theoretical underpinnings on which the techniques are based. It is important to remember that this book introduces an approach to psychotherapy and is not intended to prepare anyone to apply the techniques described. Hopefully, though, the theoretical model and the techniques derived from it will be helpful to practicing therapists and therapists in training.

In this chapter I will discuss in practical terms the two major elements of psychotherapy that were incorporated in the theoretical model: (1) working in the conflict region and (2) the nature of the relationship. The human exchange called psychotherapy, however, is rich and complex and involves more than these two major elements; in later chapters I will describe adjunctive techniques and special problems and will specify when these techniques are inappropriate.

Working in the conflict region

You will remember that the original purpose of my theoretical model was to account for the fact that as extensive research evidence seems to indicate, empathic behavior on the part of the therapist is differentially associated with successful therapy. The description of what it means to work in the conflict region will thus draw heavily on what it means to be empathic. In theoretical terms, working in the conflict region means responding to the cues of the client's conflict at the most anxiety-provoking level the client has attempted to approach himself. In translating this task into behavior, I must acknowledge a great debt to Rogers. For example, he writes (1962), "To sense the client's inner world of private personal meanings as if it were your own but without ever losing the 'as if' quality: this is empathy and this seems essential to a growth-promoting relationship. . . . When the client's world is clear to the counselor and he can move about in it freely, then he can both communicate his understanding of *what is vaguely known to the client* and he can also voice meanings in the client's experience *of which the client is scarcely aware*" (p. 419; italics added). In this last sentence Rogers seems to be describing the process of working at the "leading edge" of what the client is trying to explore. Coining descriptive phrases is sometimes dangerous, since if often leads to distorted understandings, but the phrases "leading empathy," "exploring empathy," and perhaps "deep empathy" capture some of the process I am trying to describe.

An active process. Working in the conflict region requires hard work on the part of the therapist. He is engaged in an *active* process, but he is not directing the client or attempting to "teach him the truth." "Active" means that the therapist is listening attentively, always looking for the nuances of the experiences the client is trying to communicate, and that he is *frequently* attempting to communicate his understanding of the territory the client is trying to explore. A painful development for Rogers has been the frequent misunderstanding of the nature of empathy as a passive waiting for the client to say something and using a "wooden technique of pseudo-understanding in which the counselor reflects back what the client has just said." Rogers (1962) goes on to say "I have been more than a little horrified at the interpretation of my approach which has sometimes crept into the teaching and training of counselors" (p. 420). The empathic therapist is actively and attentively involved in the exploring process in therapy.

What is the client trying to say and can't quite say? Listening to the client with this question in mind is sometimes helpful in deciding how to respond most empathically to what the client is saying. In theoretical terms, whatever the client can't quite say is the material at the "leading edge" of the conflict region—that is, at the leading edge of the client's message. The therapist is continually trying to grasp what it's like inside for his client. What is the inner flavor and what are the precisely unique meanings that the client's experience has for him? What is it that he is trying to say and can't quite say?

Dependable empathy and differential responding. The theoretical model tells us that therapeutic progress takes place most effectively when the client is trying to explore what hurts or is attempting to approach difficult material. If the therapist is successful in helping him explore difficult material, therapeutic progress will most effectively follow. It is important, however, that the therapist respond to more than just attempts to explore difficult material. The therapist's job is to demonstrate his ability and willingness to understand *all* the messages the client brings to him. The therapist is continually attentive to the client's attempts to approach difficult material, but he must also let the client learn that he can expect dependable empathy and "prizing" from his therapist. This dependable quality of the therapist's behavior is probably what lays the groundwork to free the client so that he can explore difficult areas. It is likely that good therapists do respond differentially to what their clients say, since it would be impossible to respond to all that a client brings to therapy, but this is not to say that therapists should differentially reward material they want to hear and punish, perhaps through silence, material they don't want to hear. Rather they are dependably and continuously empathic but especially attentive to self-exploratory attempts on the client's part. That is, they differentially reward different kinds of client behavior. Truax (1966), for example, has analyzed some of

Rogers' tapes and reported evidence suggesting that Rogers provided differential levels of the therapeutic conditions such as empathy or warmth for different subclasses of client behavior.

Rogers (1951, 1962) and others maintain that empathy and warmth are attitudinal variables and should therefore not be provided differentially to the client; they should not be made conditional on the client's behavior. It does seem important that the therapist's empathy and acceptance of the client be dependable and consistent, but even if they are primarily attitudinal these elements are communicated through behavior. It is probably most useful for the therapist to admit to himself that he will express his behaviors differentially, since he can't respond to everything the client provides. By recognizing that he does respond differentially the therapist can more clearly specify for himself what it is that he responds to. He can then provide for the client both selective responding (perhaps more responses to self-exploratory attempts) and an overall but perhaps less intense level of understanding of *all* that the client says.

Enriching experience.   Our discussion of neurosis noted that much neurotic behavior is influenced by conditioned reactions that are not verbalized or, because of partial repression, are incompletely verbalized. Neurotic problems consist of both cognitive elements (that is, verbalized elements) and emotive elements (non-verbalized or conditioned elements), and the reversal of the neurotic process seems to involve both cognitive (rational) activities and emotional (reconditioning) experiences. This analysis underlies an important aspect of the therapist's task. In order to help the client explore what hurts and therefore help him go through a reconditioning process, the therapist *enriches the client's experience.* He helps him explore new experiences and taste the unique felt nuances that are part of the client's life. Enriching experience often involves reliving emotional moments or feeling for the first time emotions that should have been felt before. Rice (1965; Rice & Wagstaff, 1967) has reported research evidence linking some measures of successful therapeutic outcome with both therapists' and clients' use of "expressive" emotive words, word combinations, and voice quality. "Garden variety" speech patterns were less associated with successful therapeutic outcome. They were, perhaps, less experience enriching. Where a "garden variety" therapist might say, "I guess you feel overly dependent on her," an experience-enriching therapist could express the client's message more precisely and feelingfully with, "I guess you feel like her puppy dog . . . and that hurts." One "catch phrase" that has been widely quoted as descriptive of client-centered therapy describes the therapist's task as the "reflection of feelings." Rogers (1942, 1951) has stressed the importance of responding to the emotional aspect of the client's message rather than seeing the task of therapy as entirely one of rational analysis and responding primarily to the content of what is being said. The verbal content is a necessary vehicle for communication in therapy, but the therapist must never lose sight of the fact that the leading edge of the conflict region is emotion laden. Neurotic problems contain both emotional and rational elements, and the therapist must be continuously attuned to the emotional significance of what is being said to him.

Responding to the whole message. Assuming that a good relationship exists, the therapist's task is to respond to as much of the "truth" (elements of the client's conflicts) as the client has been able to bear to approach himself. The therapist's job is to hear what the client is trying to say and can't quite say and then to help him say it. The client's attempts to communicate are sometimes only partially verbal; the therapist's job is to hear all of the client's message and to respond to it. It is when the therapist can do this that the client feels most deeply understood. *The client's message consists of all of the "signs" that the client sees as signs.* These can include non-verbal cues such as posture, tone of voice, and information previously given to the therapist. Empathic communication involves more than responding simply to what the client has just said; it involves hearing the intent of the client, hearing the signs that the client intends as signs. The therapist's task is to hear *what is implicit in the client's current experiencing*—what the client is trying to say and can't quite say.

The therapist's thoughts. The therapist is a fellow searcher whose job is to help the client explore. He is the most intent of listeners, and when he hears the client struggling to take a step he helps by taking that step with the client. When he is not sure he has heard correctly he may ask an *empathic question* such as "are you saying . . ." or he may make an *empathic guess* such as "I'm not sure this is what you mean but it's sort of a sense of. . . ." Empathic questions are not attempts at gathering information; they are attempts to communicate an understanding of the client's message. Empathic guesses are not interpretations; they are attempts to explore the edges of what the client is trying to say.

The therapist is often capable of deriving theoretical-dynamic formulations of the nature of his client's problems. Because of any or all of a number of factors—expert training in psychopathology, greater emotional health, lack of personal involvement in the problems—the therapist sometimes sees elements of the client's "painful truth" before the client does. This ability on the therapist's part can be both helpful and detrimental to the process of therapy. It can be helpful when it makes the therapist a more attentive listener. It helps him understand better where it is that the client has to go and it may attune the therapist to listen for the client's attempts to deal with particularly difficult subjects. If the therapist's diagnostic expertise helps him hear the client's message earlier than he otherwise would have, it can facilitate therapy. The therapist's expertise, however, can also be detrimental. If, in his own thinking, he becomes committed to one particular theoretical-dynamic formulation of the client's problems, he can be so eager to confirm his own formulation that he creates a self-fulfilling prophecy by leading the client to agree with him. To the extent that the therapist's formulation is incorrect, it can also prevent his hearing the client's attempts to say things that are inconsistent with the therapist's analysis. It is a sobering thought that the therapist's formulation is always doomed to be at least partially incorrect. No one is so wise that he can accurately formulate the precise nature of another person's experience. The therapist must humbly and continuously revise his understanding of any particular client and he must use whatever expert knowledge he thinks he has to hear the client better. If the therapist's formulation *is* correct, he can be sure that the client will attempt to approach the elements of his own conflict—because of the approach tendency involved in the conflict—and the therapist's job is to hear that attempt on the client's part. For many therapists the temptation to teach is nearly irresistible. When they have seen a part of the "truth" that the client is still denying, the temptation is strong to point this out to the client. Even assuming that the therapist is entirely correct (which he never is), it is not the truth that makes the client free; it is the process of finding the truth that both frees him from specific anxieties and prepares him to handle future anxieties. Telling a client the truth about himself may lead to an intellectual understanding, or at least to a professed understanding, but not to the emotional changes that are the task of therapy. Nearly all therapists have faced the client who says, "Okay, I understand my problem but I still feel bad about it, so what do I do now?"

Operationalizing the conflict region.   The leading edge of the conflict region consists of material the client is trying to communicate but hasn't quite verbalized—content and feeling that are *implicit in the message the client is intending to communicate.* Working in the conflict region means the same thing as being deeply empathic, and probably the most helpful way to operationalize what this means in behavior is to draw upon the attempts made to develop scales that rate empathy as communicated by therapists. Several empathy scales have been developed and validated (Truax & Carkhuff, 1967; Rogers, Gendlin, Kiesler, & Truax, 1967; Carkhuff & Berenson, 1967), but I will draw most heavily from Carkhuff's (1969) five-point scale, which reduces some of the ambiguity of previous scales and is designed to be applicable to all human relations.[1] The scale is based on observable behaviors, so that raters listening to tape recordings can reliably judge the degree of empathy being communicated, and this behavioral focus is also helpful to the person attempting to learn how to be empathic.

Levels 1 and 2 describe nonempathic behavior, so we will discuss them later. Level 3 is what I would call a response right at or slightly behind the conflict region, where the therapist responds only to the explicitly stated content and feeling of the client's response. Levels 4 and 5 describe functioning in the conflict region.

Level 3. The expressions of the first person (therapist) in response to the expressed feelings of the second person(s) (client) are essentially *interchangeable* with those of the second person in that they express essentially the same affect and meaning [Carkhuff, 1969, p. 316].

The therapist is responding to the surface expressions only and either does not hear or ignores feelings implicit in the client's response. This description fits the stereotype client-centered ther-

[1]From Carkhuff, R. R. *Helping and Human Relationships.* New York: Holt, Rinehart & Winston, 1969. Reprinted by permission.

apist who seems to misunderstand Rogers so thoroughly. I have noted that deep empathy is sometimes inappropriate, especially early in therapy, and level 3 responses are often necessary—to demonstrate the therapist's interest in a nonthreatening way and to set the stage for later exploration. In the next chapter, though, I will argue that the therapist who always responds at this level will have disappointing results.

Level 4. The responses of the first person add noticeably to the expressions of the second person(s) in such a way as to express feelings a level deeper than the second person was able to express himself [p. 316].

Here the therapist is adding at least something new from what was implicit in the client's intended message. The therapist must have been able to hear what the client was *trying* to say.

The client might have said, for example, "When I left home, my mother didn't even say goodby." A level 3 response to the explicit content might have been, "Not even a goodby—at a time when goodby's were called for." The more deeply empathic therapist, however, would have responded to the whole message, no doubt including nonverbal messages we can't capture on paper. A level 4 response might have added whatever feeling was implicit in the message, such as, ". . . and you felt like she should have . . . you felt she sort of left you feeling alone and a little hurt that she couldn't even say goodby."

Level 5. The first person's responses add significantly to the feeling and meaning of the expressions of the second person(s) in such a way as to (1) accurately express feelings levels below what the person himself was able to express or (2) in the event of ongoing deep self-exploration on the second person's part, to be fully with him in his deepest moments [p. 317].

In the context of our theoretical model, level 4 and level 5 responses are both within the conflict region. The difference between them is sometimes based on the amount of feeling and meaning added by the therapist; in level 4 he adds "noticeably" and in level 5 he adds "significantly." This distinction often must be made arbitrarily, since 4 and 5 are on a continuum. A level 5 response, though, is one that brings the client's message to life, restating it with precision, deep feeling, and the unique nuances that are part of the client's experience. The crucial issue is that level 5 responses must still be responses to the client's intended communication if they are to be defined as empathic. Going beyond the client's intended communication is going beyond the conflict region. Accurate level 5 responses may be the most therapeutic, but they require considerable finesse at hearing the client.

When he goes beyond the conflict region, the therapist begins to respond from his own preconceived notions and enters what I would call interpretations and level 1 on the empathy scale. Working ahead of the conflict region involves the therapist's directing the course of therapy—introducing new material, pointing out inconsistencies, contradicting the client, suggesting explanations that the client hasn't suggested, and using similar techniques. We will discuss the consequences of the therapist's working ahead of the conflict region in the next chapter. Carkhuff's level 1 definition is:

Level 1. The verbal and behavioral expressions of the first person either *do not attend* to or *detract significantly* from the verbal and behavioral expressions of the second person(s) in that they communicate significantly less of the second person's feelings than the second person has communicated himself . . . The first person may be bored or uninterested or simply operating from a preconceived frame of reference which totally excludes that of the other person(s) [p. 315].

I would characterize this level 1 response as simply not an example of empathy, but rather as interpretation or therapist-controlled direction of the process. A level 2 response, in contrast, acknowledges the client's response but either reduces its intensity or distorts it somewhat. Level 2 responses strike me as "dampening" responses that are clearly behind the conflict region.

Level 2. While the first person responds to the expressed feelings of the second person(s), he does so in such a way that *subtracts noticeable affect from the communications* of the second person. The first person may communicate some awareness of obvious surface feelings of the second person but his communications drain off a level of the affect and distort the level of meaning. The first person may communicate his own ideas of what may be going on but these are not congruent with expressions of the second person [p. 315].

The key issue in defining a response as empathic is deciding whether the therapist is *communicating understanding of the client's intended message.*

Experienced therapists often seem to hear more of the client's message than do inexperienced therapists, and one very helpful experience for any therapist is to listen to recordings of himself and others and to use the empathy rating scale to sharpen his conception of what empathy is operationally and to increase his own ability to hear the implicit message that is being communicated.

Empathy and interpretation. My theoretical model provides a framework for understanding the central therapeutic process, whether its description is couched in the terms of Rogers, of the psychoanalysts, or of other writers. Fiedler (1951) reported evidence that in their actual behaviors experienced therapists of different schools were more similar to each other than they were to novice therapists within their own theoretical orientations. The implication Fiedler drew was that regardless of one's early theoretical training, the experience of doing therapy teaches therapists what is effective and what isn't, so that in actual behavior therapists became more similar with experience. Other evidence (Strupp, 1955a, 1955b, 1957) suggests that Fiedler's analysis may apply to some behaviors and not to others, since there clearly are procedural differences among experienced therapists in different schools of psychotherapy. As my theoretical model was being developed, however, I discovered striking examples from the writings of non-Rogerian therapists that seemed to fit the theoretical model. I started out to explain the mechanism by which empathy might be therapeutic; as the model developed it became clear that a particular kind of searching or deep empathy is most effective and is most consistent with Rogers' writing. Others, however, seemed to be attempting to describe a similar process, but differences in language used and in the formulation of the therapist's role made the differences among the schools seem larger than was actually the case, at least as exemplified by therapist behavior. Quotations from a variety of therapists will illustrate the kinds of therapist behavior that seem to be descriptions of therapists' functioning at the leading edge of the conflict region.

Rogers (1942) says:

The point of view has been stressed that the counselor must be alert indeed to be responsive to the client's feelings. It should also be emphasized that only those feelings should be verbally recognized which have been expressed. Often the client has attitudes which are implied in what he says or which the counselor through shrewd observation judges him to have. *Recognition of such attitudes which have not yet appeared in the client's conversation may, if the attitudes are not too deeply repressed, hasten the progress of therapy.* If, however, they are repressed attitudes, their recognition by the counselor may seem to be very much of a threat to the client, may create resentment and resistance and in some instances may break off the counseling contacts [Italics added, p. 173].

In this quotation from his early writings, Rogers seems to be saying that responses to some feelings that have not been explicitly verbalized may be therapeutic, but he does not specify how the therapist tells what is "too deeply repressed." In Rogers' later writings it is clear that the most effective therapeutic response sometimes includes feelings that have not been verbalized but that are a part of the client's message. He also cites an unpublished description of the "nondirective attitude," written by Raskin.

Counselor participation becomes an active experiencing with the client of the feelings to which he gives expression. The counselor makes a maximum effort to get under the skin of the person with whom he's communicating, he tries to get *within* and to live the attitudes expressed instead of observing them, to catch every nuance of their changing nature; in a word, to absorb himself completely in the attitudes of the other. And in struggling to do this, there is simply no room for any other type of counselor activity or attitude; if he is attempting to live the attitudes of the other, he cannot be diagnosing them, he cannot be thinking of making the process go faster. Because he is another, and not the client, the understanding is not spontaneous but must be acquired, and this through the most intense, continuous and active attention to the feelings of the other, to the exclusion of any other type of attention [Rogers, 1951, p. 29].[2]

Rogers goes on to point out that Raskin's description does not imply an emotional identification with the client but rather an empathic identification that does not lose the "as if" quality of empathy. Raskin has vividly described the intense, attentive listening required of the therapist if he is to hear the client attempt to take a step into conflictual material. We might describe this process as an "exploring empathy."

Much psychoanalytic writing is concerned primarily with theoretical formulations rather than with specific therapeutic

[2]From Rogers, C. R. *Client-centered therapy.* Boston: Houghton Mifflin, 1951. Reprinted by permission.

techniques. One exception to this is on the timing of interpretations; many analysts say that interpretations are best delivered at the "preconscious" level. This phrase has meant different things to different theoreticians but a quotation from Menninger (1958) is, from my point of view, especially striking. He says, "It is helpful to some young analysts to have it put thus: One tells a patient what the patient *almost* sees for himself and one tells him in such a way that the patient—not the analyst—takes the 'credit' for the discovery" (p. 134). I have taken this quotation out of context, and Menninger would sharply disagree with me on many issues of therapeutic strategy, but his description of the timing of interpretations is remarkably similar to the process I have been describing. The sharpest difference, of course, lies between Menninger's view of the therapist's role as the expert who really brings out the truth and my view that the client is capable of finding the truth with a specific kind of help from the therapist; the client truly does deserve the credit for his discovery. Reik (1948), also a psychoanalyst, describes a similar process and even more explicitly casts the therapist in the expert role.

Experience of analysis gives a kind of rule of interpretation, a safeguard against acting unreasonably. I got it from Freud and have made it my own. Do not interpret until the patient himself is near to discovering the interpretation for himself, till, so to speak, he need only take one step more in order to find it himself. This final step the patient does not take alone, or, at least, very rarely. The analyst must help him to cross the threshold. Counsel is good, but it is not enough [p. 320].

My disagreement with Reik, of course, is only that the client *will* take that final step if the therapist is attentive enough to hear him trying to do so. If the therapist does not hear this attempt, the client will, as he has in the past, back off from the anxiety-provoking material he has exposed himself to.

Fenichel's psychoanalytic writing was the basis of a study done by Speisman (1959), in which he reported evidence that "moderately deep" interpretations were more often followed by client self-exploration than were either superficial or very deep interpretations. Speisman's rationale (which reflected a misunderstanding of Rogers' writings, by the way) was based on "Fenichel's advice to interpret just beyond the preconscious and Rogers' suggestions to reflect and clarify only what the patient has already stated.

Fenichel and Rogers, however, reach agreement in their opposition to even judicious use of deep interpretations" (Speisman, 1959). Fenichel's advice was that "We should avoid too deep and too superficial interpretations. When is an interpretation too deep? When the patient cannot recognize its correctness by experiencing the impulse in question" (1941). Although this may be distorting Fenichel's intent, his description seems clearly consistent with the formulation of the leading edge of the conflict region. Fenichel continues:

When so-called too deep interpretations, that is, the naming of unconscious processes which the patient cannot feel within himself, nevertheless show results, such results can be nothing else but "unspecific" ones; in other words, results that are independent of whether the interpretation is "correct" and that come about through nonanalytic changes in the dynamics of the patient. They can, for example, be results of a seduction which lies in the fact that what is otherwise taboo is being spoken about. In favorable cases such seduction can lead to diminution of anxiety and therewith to the production of less distorted derivatives; in unfavorable cases it can lead to aggravation of the fear of instinct and strengthening of the defense. But even in the most favorable case, such a decrease of anxiety, which rests only on the fact that the analyst also did something taboo, can last only as long as the analyst keeps doing this and, as in hypnosis, as long as the rapport remains unclouded. *By no means* is such an "interpretation" an interpretation in the true analytic sense, which is a real confrontation of the experiencing ego with something which it had previously warded off.

When is an interpretation too superficial? When because of the analyst's fear of affect it in some ways plays along with the patient's efforts to cover up his affects [pp. 45–46].[3]

Fenichel's other writings clearly indicate that he would advocate a much more directive and leading role for the therapist than the one I am proposing as maximally effective. I have quoted him at such length, however, because of the apparent similarity between the process he described and the analysis of working in the conflict region. Fromm-Reichmann (1950), also differing on many aspects of therapy, made an interesting comment when she said:

At the turn of the century . . . it was thought that any psychiatrist who was emotionally stable, was well trained in the use of psychotherapeutic

[3]From Fenichel, O. Problems of psychoanalytic technique. Albany, N. Y.: *Psychoanalytic Quarterly*, 1941. Reprinted by permission.

tools, and showed integrity and medical responsibility could treat any type of patient. We know now that the success or failure of psychoanalytic psychotherapy is, in addition, greatly dependent upon the question of whether or not there is an empathic quality between the psychiatrist and the patient [p. 62].

One especially interesting quotation is from Cameron (1963), who says:

The good therapist does not of course coerce his patient to move too rapidly into sensitive areas. As French has often expressed it, the good therapist, like the good gardener, waits until he recognizes something which is struggling to emerge and then makes it easier for it to emerge. He never tries to drag anything up from the unconscious or deep preconscious into awareness [p. 769].

We could hardly hope for a more succinct description of the therapist's task.

The therapeutic relationship

Saying that the therapist's task is to create a "good relationship" before therapeutic growth can take place means that his goal is to create an atmosphere that is both nonthreatening and somehow socially rewarding to the client. Describing the way this can be accomplished is an overwhelmingly complicated task. One's understanding of the process of establishing a good relationship depends upon reading much of the massive amount written about forming relationships. It depends even more on experience in establishing relationships in psychotherapy and probably still more on experience as a human being in relationships with other human beings. It is discomforting but true that the ability to form good relationships depends on many things that no teacher can teach and no book can explain. Our task is not hopeless, however, and in the rest of this chapter I will describe some of the major elements of a good relationship and will refer to several references that treat the therapeutic relationship more thoroughly.

A relationship consists of behaviors that mutually affect two or more people. The therapist's task is to create a rewarding, nonthreatening atmosphere, and the behaviors that will create such an atmosphere differ from client to client. There do seem, however, to be some kinds of relationship behaviors that are rewarding and nonthreatening to most clients. Many people have attempted to define what these common factors are. Shoben (1949), for example, says:

The most underscored aspect of the therapeutic relationship seems to be its warmth, permissiveness, and complete freedom from moralistic and judgmental attitudes on the part of the counselor. Far from being a coldly objective consideration of the patient's troubles, therapy necessarily involves a highly personal form of interaction in which the counselor is highly acceptant of the client's behavior, both overt and covert within clearly defined limits . . . An atmosphere free from censure-like judgment but pervaded by sympathetic understanding is provided by the counselor. On the other hand, acceptance does not imply approval of the client's feelings, attitudes, or overt behavior. This is not surprising since most clinical cases hardly approve of themselves and their self-disapproval provides one of the most important aspects of the discomfort that brings them into therapy [p. 374].

A considerable amount of research evidence has been reported to relate successful therapy with the therapist's communication of "nonpossessive warmth" (Truax & Carkhuff, 1967). The phrase "nonpossessive warmth" is an adaptation of Rogers' earlier use of the phrase "unconditional positive regard." The word "unconditional" has led to considerable misunderstanding of this concept, since the conduct of therapy is generally conditional upon the establishment of certain limits, to be discussed later. However, what Rogers means is that within the limits of the therapy situation the therapist's caring for and being interested in and prizing of the client are not conditional on the client's producing feelings and thoughts that are acceptable to the therapist. The therapist does not attack his client in a judgmental way, but he must do more than simply not attack; he must communicate a basic attitude of interest in and concern for his client. The key issue seems to be that the client must learn that the therapist is a *dependable* source of prizing acceptance. He must learn that no matter what he says the therapist will continue to be interested in him and see him as a worthwhile person. Presumably, the good parent communicates to his child, "There are limits to your behaviors which must be observed but you are free to have all of your feelings and thoughts and still be a worthwhile, good, lovable person." In Chapter 3 internalized conflicts were discussed as the major source of anxiety and low self-esteem. What the conflicted person has learned is that his own impulses and feelings are "bad"; that is, the impulses and feelings themselves have become *punishers*—cues for fear. Such a person comes to think of himself as the source of his own "badness." The therapist is communicating, "Your thoughts and feelings are legitimate, acceptable, and you are free to deal with them." The therapist, like the good parent, sets certain limits on behavior, but within the therapy hours he permits free exploration of thoughts and feelings. The previously punishing thoughts and feelings lose their status as fear cues. What the client *is* loses its "badness."

The client has come to expect social punishment for being what he is. The therapist must communicate to him a dependable non-punishment and, even more, a dependable acceptance in response to the client's being what he is. The client must build up expectations of trust in the responses of the therapist. To build such expectations requires repeated frequent experiences of receiving the therapist's prizing. The client must repeatedly experience having his responses followed by the therapist's dependable respect for him as a person.

It might be useful to be able to provide a list of behaviors for communicating nonpossessive warmth, respect, prizing, and dependable acceptance, but even if that were possible such a list would probably have both good and bad effects on the therapist. The ability to communicate a dependable acceptance to another person depends more on whether the therapist is really interested in what the client is saying. Can he really hear the client and does he work hard at helping explore what the client needs to explore? Does he really care whether the client hurts or not? These are the feelings and attitudes that lead to the expression of dependable nonpossessive warmth far more reliably than the application of behavioral rules.

In addition to not being very helpful, a list of behaviors would probably be impossible to compile. As Truax and Carkhuff (1967) have said:

A careful cataloguing of the kinds of behaviors and verbalizations that people use to communicate warmth or positive regard could easily fill a number of books. Even in the more limited relationship of counseling and of psychotherapy, warmth and respect can be communicated or not communicated by the therapist in a variety of ways. . . . Because of the many different ways in which individuals communicate and interpret the communication of non-possessive warmth, the therapist must inevitably rely heavily upon his accurate, empathic understanding of the client to sense the mode and the content that will communicate his positive caring or warmth most effectively [p. 314].

In this chapter we are interested in "real life" applications of relationships and must recognize the inadequacy of our understanding of the complexities of human interaction. For purposes of research, however, we must try to specify a limited number of observable behaviors as constituting "good relationships." Good "first approximations" of attempts to do this have been reported (Rogers, Gendlin, Kiesler, & Truax, 1967; Truax & Carkhuff, 1967). These rating scales are based on observable behaviors such as "actively approving or disapproving" (setting conditions), responding "mechanically," and showing "passivity" and "lack of interest" at the low end of the scale, as compared with "deep interest and concern" shown "without conditions" at the high end.

Working in the conflict region is therapeutically effective only in the presence of a good relationship (that is, a counterconditioning agent). Deep empathy or consistent responding in the conflict region alone may be detrimental, since holding the client in the presence of anxiety-provoking cues without reducing that anxiety can make the therapist and therapy situation themselves anxiety cues and punish the client for his approach behavior. Early in therapy the central task, then, is to communicate nonpossessive warmth and respect to the client and to provide repeated experiences in which the client's responses are followed by understanding and acceptance of a nonthreatening nature. Nonleading empathy responses can communicate, "I am listening to you, I am interested in what you are saying, and I will continue to respond to you in this way no matter what you choose to discuss. At this moment my total concern is for you as a person." These messages are most effectively communicated by the therapist's behavior. The client learns that the therapist's understanding, interest, and acceptance are dependable through repeated experiences of their consistency. Occasionally therapists express their caring for their client verbally, but this is a tricky business and must be done very judiciously. One danger is that, especially early in therapy, an open statement of caring or liking may be difficult for the client

to believe because of his previous experiences with social relationships and because of his feeling that the therapist can't possibly
know him well enough to make such a statement sincerely. In
addition, many clients have experienced the verbalization of being
liked associated with subtle forms of rejection, and the words "I
like you" may be perceived as quite threatening. Keeping these
cautions in mind, the therapist can use verbal expressions of caring
for a client, but he can probably communicate interest and respect
more effectively by acting interested and respecting.

Recently Rogers (1962) has placed more and more importance on
the therapist's congruence as a therapeutic agent. Rogers sees the
effective therapeutic agents as empathy, unconditional positive
regard, and congruence. My model includes both unconditional
positive regard and congruence as factors that contribute to the
therapeutic relationship. The congruent therapist is in touch with
his own feelings and is honest about his feelings in relationship to
his client. His honesty in the relationship means that he avoids
being "phony." The therapist must encounter the client as a complete and real human being. However, the notion of congruence
raises some problems for the creation of an effective therapeutic
relationship. One thorny and hopefully infrequent problem arises
when the therapist dislikes his client—a circumstance that only
the godlike can always avoid. There seems to be no easy answer
to such a problem, since the open expression of dislike might be
expected to be detrimental to the client's anxiety problems (a
further reinforcement of what others have done to him); but trying
to play-act a caring for the client may create detrimental phoni-
ness. Even the usually suggested transfer to another therapist can
be perceived by the client as a form of rejection and be detrimental
to him. Hopefully, the therapist will be a tolerant and accepting
enough person that this situation is rare; there seems to be no
entirely satisfactory solution to it. Another aspect of congruence
worth discussing here is that of expressing negative feelings to a
client toward whom the therapist is generally accepting, prizing,
and respecting. Such expression can be useful *provided* that the
client has built up a strong enough expectation of trust in the
therapist's acceptance of him. The expression of anger, for example, can be useful if the client is capable of learning the lesson that
the expression of anger is not equivalent to the withdrawal of love
or acceptance—a lesson that the good parent presumably teaches
his child.

Transference. The psychoanalytic term "transference" refers to the *irrational* reactions of the client to the therapist, as though the therapist were some previous person in the client's experience. To a large extent, of course, all relationships are based on previous experiences with people and in that sense are transferred through the process of generalization, a point made most explicitly by Dollard and Miller (1950). Seen in this light, however, transference loses any special meaning, since all relationships are based on such generalizations. In fact, it is common to misunderstand transference as *any* positive or negative feelings the client has for the therapist. To have any usefulness, the term "transference" should apply only to strong emotional reactions with no apparent basis in reality. There is little doubt that such reactions occur sometimes, and all therapists should be familiar with the psychoanalytic literature on transference. There is a danger, however, in looking upon the therapeutic relationship as a transference relationship, as opposed to a "real" relationship. When a true—that is, irrational—transference does occur it should be seen as a "symptom," a way of avoiding anxiety, and should be dealt with in therapy as any other problem would be dealt with. The therapist must be careful that he does not mechanize and distance himself from the therapy relationship by thinking of it as "simply a transference situation." Such an attitude can be a strategy by which the therapist avoids encountering the client, perhaps because of his own inability to participate in the relationship. Moreover, when transference does become a problem the difficulty may lie partly with the client and partly with the therapist. Butler (1952) has made the point that in classical analysis the therapist creates a permissive atmosphere during early free association and then in the later interpretive phases of therapy he becomes authoritarian and parent-like. Butler has argued that such behavior on the therapist's part *elicits* "transference reactions," since the client has no other techniques for dealing with parent-like authorities.

Countertransference. "Countertransference" refers to the irrational aspects (that is, not realistically based on the present situation) of the therapist's reaction to the client. As with transference, countertransference is often misused to refer to any positive or negative feelings the therapist has for his client. This too can become the therapist's way of saying that therapy is not a "real" relationship. As with transference, however, real (irrational) countertransference does occur sometimes, and the therapist must be alert to any of his own feelings that seem unusually strong or seem based on very limited contact with a particular client. The therapist should also be alert for a more subtle kind of problem that could be classed as a form of countertransference: the extent to which his own personal problems hamper his ability to hear what his client is trying to say. There is evidence (Bergin, 1966) that the emotionally healthy therapist is more effective. There are, of course, many reasons why this is true, but one certainly is that the more emotionally healthy therapist is more open to his own experience and more able to hear all of his client's experience. We all lie to ourselves, and it is incumbent upon the therapist to maintain a continual check on himself to be sure that his own problems are not interfering with his effectiveness as a therapist. For this reason, many therapists have found it especially beneficial to have received psychotherapy themselves, and it is a common practice for a therapist to have a colleague with whom his sole relationship is to discuss his own ability as a person to deal with psychotherapy clients.

Frieda Fromm-Reichmann (1950) commented that therapy seems to require "empathic matches" between therapist and client. The reason that some therapist-client pairs are more effective than others is undoubtedly related at least in part to the therapist's ability to hear and deal with specific kinds of problems. Part of the therapist's job is to be an attentive listener. It is his responsibility to maintain a continuous check on his own ability to hear.

Limits of the therapy relationship. The good therapist provides his client with remarkably attentive listening, intensely worked-at understanding, and unusually dependable respect and acceptance. He provides the client freedom to deal with all of his thoughts and feelings. The therapist provides these qualities at a level that he as a human being would be unable to maintain continuously. The reason for setting limits in psychotherapy is to prohibit behaviors and demands upon the therapist that would prevent him from being able to provide the understanding and acceptance that are the central ingredients of psychotherapy. The client must not, for example, harm the therapist physically, and this knowledge frees both the therapist and the client to deal openly with feelings and thoughts of hostility toward the therapist. The client is permitted only a limited segment of the therapist's time, and this knowledge frees the therapist to provide an intensity of acceptance and listening he could not maintain if he was unsure that the demands made on him would be limited. Many limits of psychotherapy are widely agreed upon, but some are idiosyncratic to specific therapists. With some therapists, for example, the implications and possible consequences of physical touching in therapy create such an uncertain difficulty that such touching is beyond the agreed-upon limits of the relationship. Other therapists do not feel the need to set this particular limit.

Although the primary function of limits is to permit the therapist to function more fully as a therapist, a second function is to provide the client with a similar reality-based structure that frees him to deal more fully with thoughts and feelings, knowing that both he and the therapist are prohibited from acting in certain ways on those thoughts and feelings.

Other "therapeutic" relationships. Many characteristics differentiate the therapy relationship from other relationships: therapy is less reciprocal than most relationships, it is bound by relatively clearly defined limits, and it is more intense and concentrated than most other relationships. The principles, however, that make therapy therapeutic are the same principles that govern the effects other relationships have on the participants. Therapy's task, in one sense, is to undo the damage of past poor relationships that have taught the client, often in several insidious ways, that his thoughts and feelings and impulses are bad, that he is bad and unworthy. Therapy follows a continuous course of reconditioning the client through the process we have been discussing. Any relationship, however, that provides a person with understanding and acceptance can accomplish the goals we have set for therapy. Love relationships often make the participants more emotionally healthy. This is not always the case, of course, but any relationship marked by understanding and acceptance should be therapeutic, and it is certainly this observation that led Schofield (1964) to entitle his book *Psychotherapy: The Purchase of Friendship*. Presumably if each of us had relationships characterized by empathic understanding and thoroughly dependable acceptance, psychotherapists would all be forced into other lines of work.

6

The effects of therapy

In my outline of the nature of neurosis in Chapter 3, I described four problems that the client typically brings to psychotherapy: anxiety, symptoms, impaired problem-solving ability, and low self-esteem.[1] This chapter specifies the ways that empathy-oriented therapy alleviates these problems. By stating therapy's goals within these four broad categories, I have created a conceptually clean task in this chapter. I am begging several questions, however —questions for which I have no satisfactory answers. Any decision about what constitutes a desirable outcome for a particular client must be, in part, a value judgment, and the question of values has created difficulty in every attempt to study and understand the nature of healthy personality. Judgments about what is neurotic are relative within every culture, and the area of values and emotional health is fraught with questions such as, "In a 'sick'

[1]After an extensive review of the literature, Volsky and associates (1965) arrived at a very similar list of desired outcomes: anxiety reduction, defensiveness reduction, and an increase in problem-solving ability.

society is it neurotic to be deviant, particularly when that deviance brings suffering to oneself?" The problem becomes further complicated if one tries to define what a "sick" society is. Unless the therapist is prepared to take the responsibility for imposing his own exact value structure on all his clients, he must maintain a broad latitude within which the client is free to choose his own goals and the behaviors that will achieve those goals. The therapist's job is to free his client to make accurate use of his own experiences.

With this inadequate analysis of the problem of values and therapeutic outcome I will refer you to some more complete (but still not totally adequate) discussions of this issue (Rogers, 1961; London, 1964; Szasz, 1961; Smith, 1961) and return to the relative safety of our broadly stated goals. The client, the therapist, and others presumably are in general agreement that the client has come to therapy with "excessive" (whatever "excessive" means at that moment in that culture) anxiety, symptoms, poor problem-solving ability, and low self-esteem. These problems are primarily conflict-based, and the therapist's job is to reduce the conflicts and the four major concomitant problems to a level within what is considered normal and adaptive.

A recent and sobering observation is that of the "deterioration effect" (Bergin, 1966, 1970). Some therapists seem to be helping clients while some seem actually to be doing damage. It is the responsibility of those in the field to specify not only why therapy might help, but how it also might harm. Therefore, in this chapter I will use my theoretical model to explain possible consequences of ineffective therapy, as well as to specify the effects of successful therapy.

Anxiety reduction

The experience of anxiety is usually conflict-based, and what is reported as neurotic anxiety is usually based on internalized conflicts. The client experiences himself as the source of his own anxiety. We have traced the process by which internalized conflicts can be reduced through a step-by-step progression, as a result of the therapist's responding to the client's attempts to approach the elements of his own conflicts. When the conflicts are relieved or reduced, the reported experience of anxiety will be relieved or reduced. The anxious client comes to therapy with impulses that are internally motivated, and therefore unavoidable, but that also have acquired the properties of fear cues. The impulses are both unavoidable and punishing. Through the therapy process these impulses lose some of their fear-arousing cue properties through a process of reconditioning. The expression of these impulses is paired, in successful therapy, with social rewards, reversing the process of social punishment by which they became fear cues. Anxiety is reduced to the extent that conflict is reduced.

Therapy (conflict relief) is both a rational (verbal) and emotional (nonverbal) process, and many of the changes that occur are not the direct result of explicit verbalization. Among humans, words are an efficient vehicle for dealing with experience, and therapy is greatly enhanced by fuller verbalization of previously partially conscious material that was fear arousing ("making the unconscious conscious"). This verbalization is the most available way for the client to expose himself to the fear-arousing cues. However, much that goes on in therapy happens at a subverbal level, and it is even theoretically possible that conflict relief could take place without verbalization. The point is that verbalization is an extremely effective part of therapy but it is neither completely necessary nor sufficient for therapeutic changes to take place.

This observation can be illustrated by several possible outcomes of the hypothetical case mentioned in Chapter 3. A young man complained of the "dumb" mistakes he was making that were causing his father's business to fail. The "mistakes" were presumably the result of partially conscious feelings of hatred for the father, feelings so guilt-arousing that the young man could not acknowledge them and therefore could not deal with them adaptively. The young man might have entered therapy with an empathic therapist who enabled him to explore his thoughts and feelings and eventually verbalize his impulses, as the impulses became less fear arousing, freeing him for more adaptive problem-solving. However, there are many ways the same relief of internalized conflict could have been accomplished without verbalization. It is conceivable that the client might have expressed anger toward an older man resembling the father, or even toward the therapist, and received understanding rather than punishment in return.

Such an experience would reduce his fear of his angry impulses, and some of this reduction could easily generalize to his feelings toward his father, without the necessity for explicit verbalization of what had happened. It is even possible that the young man might have had angry impulses and thoughts about his father while sitting in that tub of warm water I mentioned in Chapter 4, which might have counterconditioned the fear of his impulses to some extent without requiring him to verbalize "what happened to make him feel better." This kind of "serendipitous" conflict relief (reconditioning) goes on all the time for all of us. Sometimes it does not happen naturally and we must arrange for it to happen by providing a specialized relationship called psychotherapy; but the principles are the same. Much of the change in therapy is also described as "just feeling better," without explicit verbalization of the process. Words are the vehicle of conflict relief in therapy, and they greatly facilitate the process, but they do not account for all the change that occurs.

In addition to the longer-term relief of anxiety as a result of conflict reduction, many clients experience, especially early in therapy, a temporary anxiety reduction that seems to be based on expectations or hopes. The self-confidence of the therapist and the suggestion that here finally lies hope for relief can exert a kind of placebo effect (Frank, 1961). This kind of anxiety relief is not necessarily related to the conflict-reduction model and its effects, and although beneficial and often useful to therapy it should be considered only temporary if the client's problems are based on internalized conflicts.

Symptom reduction

A sometimes unfriendly debate has been going on between psychoanalysts and behavior modifiers over the question of symptom substitution. Remove the symptom, say the behavior modifiers, and you have cured the neurosis (Eysenck, 1964). No, reply the psychoanalysts, the symptom is only an anxiety substitute, and if you remove the symptom without resolving the underlying psychic cause you only create the need for a new symptom. My response is that both sides are partly correct, depending on the etiology of a particular problem (Cahoon, 1968). I firmly reject the psychic-energy illness model, but the learning model predicts that if a particular maladaptive behavior still serves an anxiety-reducing function related to internalized conflicts, removing the symptom by such means as direct punishment, reciprocal inhibition, suggestion, and hypnosis leaves the client in a high drive state for which he must find some other form of relief. However, if what has been called a symptom is the result of insufficient learning experiences, if it is a directly conditioned fear, or if it is a well-reinforced habit based on a no-longer-existing conflict, then symptom-removal by direct means is an entirely adequate treatment procedure.

The issue becomes even more complicated when we recall that everyone uses anxiety-avoiding behaviors, and they become "symptoms" only when society or the individual decides that they are excessively maladaptive. This means that even where there is a strong internalized conflict, the process of removing a particular anxiety-avoiding behavior and thus forcing the individual to find a new anxiety-avoiding behavior may result in the "choice" of a less noticeable "symptom." It will appear that symptom substitution has not taken place, since this new behavior is within acceptable limits. The new anxiety-avoiding behavior might, however, be *more* noticeable and objectionable and lead observers to say that symptom substitution had indeed taken place.

Chapter 8 will specify that neurotic problems not based on internalized conflicts are appropriately treated by behavior modification. However, neurotic problems commonly involve internalized conflicts, and in these cases the removal of symptoms is contingent upon the reduction of the underlying conflict. We must be careful not to confuse the learning model of neurosis with a disease model, but it is accurate to speak of underlying causes if we understand the process by which conflict reduction reinforces anxiety-reducing behaviors. The task of therapy is to reduce the need for the symptom by reducing the conflict that creates that need. In most cases the symptom is then punished out of existence in normal interaction with the environment because it is painful and it no longer serves as the lesser of two pains.

One further thought on symptoms is that most clients come to therapy without a clear-cut set of behaviors that can be called symptoms. We have seen that the experience of anxiety is often what brings a person to therapy, but, in addition, many clients come dissatisfied and unhappy with their lives. Part of their dissatisfaction is over "stupid" things they do. They feel unable to love or they blow up too easily. They may be compulsively promiscuous but burdened with guilt, or feel detached and strange without knowing why. The possibilities are endless. Some such behaviors can probably be called symptoms, but we must be careful not to become so associated with the disease model that our view of neurosis is symptom-oriented. The behavioral causal patterns of the symptoms (the learning history that caused them) is a far more useful focus for understanding neurosis.

Problem-solving ability

Chapter 3 discussed how conflict can lead to impaired problem-solving ability because of such factors as the repression of relevant information, the constriction of cue utilization, and a reduced tendency to explore new experiences—because of the pain previously associated with such experiences. The person with neurotic problems uses the information available to him from the environment and from his own thought processes incompletely and therefore inaccurately. This leads him to be "neurotically stupid" (Dollard & Miller, 1950). Nearly all writers on the topic of neurosis have discussed this aspect of neurosis and have referred to it in different terms. Rogers, for example, speaks of a lack of "openness to experience," and Sullivan discusses "selective perception." It is clear that the person with neurotic problems does things that appear foolish to others and is perplexed by things that others think he "should" be able to figure out from the learning experiences available to him. Successful therapy enhances a client's problem-solving ability for several reasons. Much is accomplished simply through anxiety reduction and the progressively more intense discussion of previously repressed material. The client has more information available to help him make decisions.

Of longer-term importance is the fact that the effective therapist not only assists in the solution of particular problems but also helps the client discover a new mode of coping with his problems. An absolutely essential difference between the approach we have been discussing and other approaches is the insistence that therapy should be based on the client's initiative and attempts to approach his own solutions. *He must experience repeated reinforcement of his attempts to explore himself.* The client is not only having specific anxieties relieved; he is acquiring a new approach to dealing with all of his experiences, both present and future. The client must eventually leave his therapist and should be able to rely on his own resources in the future. It is the therapist's responsibility not to be an expert problem-solver for the client but to create the conditions within which the client can solve his own problems. The therapist must be careful not to encourage and reinforce dependency on his expert guidance, advice, and teaching. Creating such a dependency can turn therapy into a temporarily helpful but eventually costly lesson.

When we discuss the uses of behavior modification in Chapter 8, we will see that for reasons of economy a therapist sometimes must settle for less than all of the potential benefits of therapy. He might, for example, recondition specific anxieties through behavior modification and perhaps teach the client reconditioning techniques he can use by himself in the event of later problems; such learnings provide a limited but still desirable outcome for therapy. Eysenck (1964) has rightly pointed out, for example, that eliminating a strong anxiety can break the vicious circle of avoidance behavior, leading to further gains resulting from life experiences. Teaching the client autoconditioning techniques may be a useful adjunct to the more general benefit of enhancing his thought processes.

Self-acceptance

The etiology of low self-esteem is a learning process in which one's own behaviors and impulses have been punished so that they became fear or anxiety cues. The experience reported by the victim of such a learning history is a feeling of worthlessness.[2] The client *is* his feelings and impulses and thoughts, and these have become a source of painful emotions. What he *is* seems to him to be bad. His responses have been repeatedly punished and have, through conditioning, become punishers themselves. The reversal

[2]Feelings of worthlessness, guilt, depression, and other painful emotions are most accurately understood as forms of anxiety; they are based on conditioned conflicts. They each "feel different," however, and useful distinctions can be made among them.

of this process is accomplished in psychotherapy through the repeated rewarding of the same or similar responses, *as emitted by the client.* The key issue is that the therapist must respond, not as a leading teacher, but in relation to the client's responses. For the client to come to feel "I am good and worthwhile," he must go through repeated experiences of emitting responses that make up what he is and of having those responses associated with socially rewarding behaviors. Through this process he experiences a realization: "Here is someone (the therapist) who knows me as I am and finds me acceptable. I for some reason now feel more acceptable to myself, I feel more worthwhile. I like myself better and am therefore now less dependent on the judgments of others toward me." It seems likely that accepting oneself is dependent on, at some time, being accepted by another. This acceptance is what the emotionally healthy child receives from his parents. It is what must sometimes be provided in the therapy setting.

An interesting note on the nature of changes in self-esteem grows out of a client statement frequently reported by therapists. Clients sometimes say words such as "I really feel better about myself. I like myself better. I don't see how it could be related to therapy, though, since we have not arrived at any great insights or dramatic new understandings." The process by which anxiety is reduced and self-acceptance increased is only partially verbally mediated. Therapy is, to repeat, partially a verbal (rational) process and partially a nonverbal (emotional) process. The repeated experience of emitting responses and receiving acceptance and understanding in return can result in dramatic emotional changes that occur in small, repeated, and nearly unnoticeable steps. It is a kind of growth of which the client need not always be aware and need not always understand to benefit from, just as full verbalization is not a necessary condition for anxiety relief.

The consequences of ineffective therapy

According to the conflict-relief model, effective therapy requires that the therapist work in the conflict region, assuming that a good relationship exists. This requirement also suggests the consequences of two kinds of ineffective therapy: when the therapist usually responds "behind" the conflict region, and when the therapist is repeatedly working "ahead" of the conflict region.

To see how a therapist works behind, within, and ahead of the conflict region, we can compare three possible responses to the previously mentioned hypothetical client whose partially conscious hatred for his father led to mistakes and failure in his father's business.

Client: I usually feel that I love my father so much, there's almost nothing I wouldn't do for him ... (voice trails off uncertainly).

A response at or behind the conflict region would be essentially interchangeable with the client's response. It would be at the "minimal level of facilitative interpersonal functioning" (Carkhuff, 1969):

Therapist: Most of the time you feel that quite strongly—the desire to help him.

Responding within the conflict region, the therapist would add to the feeling and meaning by responding to both the explicit and implicit message that the client seems to intend as his message. He responds to all of the material that the client is trying to say and hasn't quite said, picking up a hint of ambivalence:

Therapist: I guess it's sort of a mixed thing for you. . . . Usually you feel that way, and sometimes your feeling is less strong. I sense some feeling of puzzlement over that.

In working ahead of the conflict region, the therapist might quite accurately see that the client's "love" for his father masks deep feelings of dislike, and he might respond with material that is not implicit in the client's intended message:

Therapist: I think your feeling is a mixture of the love you talk about and also a feeling that frightens you—a feeling of anger and hatred toward your father.

The therapist might go on to support the accuracy of his interpretation, but the crucial issue is that he has gone beyond the client's message to introduce his own preconceived frame of reference (which we are assuming for the moment is correct, in the sense of being "really true").

Responding "behind" the conflict region. A common and incorrect stereotype of the client-centered therapist is that he responds to what the client has explicitly just said. In theoretical terms, this kind of functioning should be totally ineffective. Since the anxiety cues would never be dealt with and since they would be continuously avoided, the reconditioning process associated with those cues could not take place. Actually, the stereotype client-centered therapist who works behind the conflict region probably does make some progress, but very slowly. Since clients frequently do explicitly verbalize conflict material, the therapist who responds only to these occasional explicit steps into the conflict region will still help the client make some therapeutic progress. The difficulty with this approach is that it is very slow, and the client often perceives the therapist as innanely repetitive. Rogers (1951) expresses the same thought from his own point of view when he says:

In the first place some counselors—usually those with little specific training—have supposed that the counselor's role in carrying on nondirective counseling was merely to be passive and to adopt a laissez-faire policy. Such a counselor has some willingness for the client to be self-directing. He is more inclined to listen than to guide. He tries to avoid imposing his own evaluations upon the client. He finds that a number of his clients gain help for themselves. He feels that his faith in the client's capacity is best exhibited by a passivity which involves a minimum of activity and of emotional reaction on his part. He tries "to stay out of the client's way."

This misconception of the approach has led to considerable failure in counseling—and for good reasons. In the first place, the passivity and seeming lack of interest or involvement is experienced by the client as a rejection, since indifference is in no real way the same as acceptance. In the second place, a laissez-faire attitude does not in any way indicate to the client that he is regarded as a person of worth. Hence the counselor who plays a merely passive role, a listening role, may be of assistance to some clients who are desperately in need of emotional catharsis, but by and large his results will be minimal, and many clients will leave both disappointed in their failure to receive help and disgusted with the counselor for having nothing to offer (p. 27).[3]

The therapist's role is an *active* role. Doing therapy is hard work, not a passive listening. It is an active listening for the client's attempts to deal with conflictual material.

[3]From Rogers, C. R. *Client-centered therapy.* Boston: Houghton Mifflin, 1951. Reprinted by permission.

Working "ahead" of the conflict region. Most therapists agree that passive reflection is an inappropriate approach to psychotherapy. I will get much disagreement, however, with my formulation of psychotherapy when I say that working ahead of the conflict region is also an undesirable approach. Many authorities see the ideal therapist as an expert who takes the final step for the client (Reik, 1948) or as one who directs and confronts the client with interpretations (Dollard & Miller, 1950; Ellis, 1962; Harper, 1959; Menninger, 1958). In fact, by using the conflict model, one could specify ways in which working ahead of the conflict region could result in a beneficial reconditioning of anxiety cues and an apparently dramatic progress in anxiety reduction. These benefits, however, are won at a price—a price that need not be paid if the therapist is functioning maximally within the style of therapy we have been discussing. Many therapists expose their clients to strong anxiety-provoking cues (words, thoughts, feelings) and at the same time provide effective counterconditioning agents, such as an extremely strong relationship, very convincing presentations of the therapist's own strength, and reassurance that these feelings and thoughts and words are acceptable. Such an approach could result in some reduction of anxiety, which could lead to further growth outside the therapy situation by breaking a vicious circle of avoidance behavior. This directive approach, however, lacks one of the crucial elements of empathy-based psychotherapy and may even have a detrimental effect. Empathy-based therapy involves the continuous and repeated reinforcement of the *client's approach responses.* The task of therapy is not only to relieve specific anxieties; it is to enable the client to become autonomous and strong enough to take the initiative in the resolution and avoidance of future anxieties. An ongoing goal of therapy is to provide anxiety reduction immediately following every approach response made by the client. However, if the therapist leads the client too much—that is, works ahead of the conflict region—he will be repeatedly following the client's approach responses not with anxiety reduction but with continued anxiety arousal. Although neither the therapist nor the client would verbalize the situation this way, the client will be going through repeated experiences of mild punishment for making his approach responses. This is obviously a subtle and long-term process and is often obscured by the fact that some counterconditioning may also be occurring, creating what seems at the moment to be desirable movement. But although the process may be subtle, the consequences are important. The process will teach the client that anxiety reduction is more dependent on the therapist's initiative than on his own and that his own approach responses bring pain. The client's acquiring the ability to solve his own problems depends instead on the therapist's *continuous reinforcement of the client's approach responses.*[4]

In addition, changes in self-esteem occur in subtly different ways in these two different approaches to therapy. Low self-esteem is the result of being made anxious by one's own responses, and if those responses can be counterconditioned as fear cues, an increase in self-esteem should result. Such an increase could be expected in both the empathy-based approach and in a more leading kind of therapy. An important difference, however, is that in empathy-based therapy the therapist responds to cues *emitted by and originating with the client.* It is quite possible that the *therapist* can elicit responses and then countercondition the elicited cues. If, however, the cues are counterconditioned after the client emits them, it is he who is responsible for and takes the "credit" for being the source of his responses. It is more clearly what he has done for himself that makes him feel better about himself, and he is less dependent on the therapist for this present growth and for future growth.

A further danger in working ahead of the conflict region is the establishment, through higher-order conditioning, of the therapist and the therapy situation as anxiety cues. Not only is the therapist consistently being paired with powerful anxiety cues, he is seen as the source of these cues. This creates the potential for a new conflict in which the client may fear therapy but be unable to leave it—because of the therapist's subtle pressures, society's pressures, and perhaps his own desperate need for help. The therapist can create a conflict situation which itself calls for subtle and complicated kinds of defenses. The therapist's task is to continuously reduce the client's need for his defenses, beginning in the first

---

[4]Some recent evidence (Berenson, Mitchell, & Laney, 1969) may require that I modify my criticisms of the therapist's use of confrontation (therapist's statement of disagreement with the client's perceptions of his experience). There is some suggestion that "experiential" (as opposed to "didactic") confrontations used by "high functioning" (on empathy, warmth, and congruence) therapists may be beneficial. This evidence is, at present, only suggestive. (See Chapter 7 for a fuller discussion of this issue.)

interview. If the therapist *creates* a conflict situation, he may see this reflected in a therapeutic impasse, in resistance, in negative transference, and, perhaps most dangerously, in a "flight into health." What better way to get rid of one's therapist than to "get well" quickly? Interestingly, Truax and Carkhuff (1963) have reported evidence that high levels of empathy in early therapy sessions were related to premature terminations. This finding is consistent with the counterconditioning notion and is relevant to this discussion of clients who are driven from therapy by an anxiety-arousing therapist.

One dangerous consequence of flights into health is that they provide therapists with grossly inaccurate feedback about their own effectiveness. Every therapist wants to believe that he is effective, and it is extremely difficult to face one's own therapeutic failures. It may be that clients who "get well" quickly are providing misleading reinforcement for what might well be the therapists' destructive behavior. The need for accurate feedback about one's own effectiveness creates a thorny problem for therapists. The most effective ways to prevent therapists' being deluded by their own needs, and by their clients' possibly inaccurate assessments, probably lie in the conduct of research and in continuous feedback from listening to recordings of oneself and from discussions with trusted colleagues.

A further danger in working ahead of the conflict region is the inevitable therapist error about what is true for a particular client. The comments made so far have assumed that the therapist was precisely correct in his formulation but helped the client see it too early. However, the therapist is never precisely correct, and when he makes an error he pays a price by making the client feel less well understood, by punishing the client for his approach responses, and by providing "answers" that the client may have trouble rejecting.

I am going to repeat a quotation from Fenichel (1941) that appeared in Chapter 5. In describing the consequences of a "too-deep interpretation" and in describing why such behavior sometimes seems to "work," Fenichel comes very close to saying (in analytic terminology) what I have just said about the consequences, both potentially good and bad, of working ahead of the conflict region:

When so-called too deep interpretations, that is, the naming of unconscious processes which the patient cannot feel within himself, nevertheless show results, such results can be nothing else but "unspecific" ones;
in other words, results that are independent of whether the interpretation
is "correct" and that come about through nonanalytic changes in the
dynamics of the patient. They can, for example, be results of a seduction
which lies in the fact that what is otherwise taboo is being spoken about.
In favorable cases such seduction can lead to diminution of anxiety and
therewith to the production of less distorted derivatives; in unfavorable
cases it can lead to aggravation of the fear of instinct and strengthening
of the defense. But even in the most favorable case, such a decrease of
anxiety, which rests only on the fact that the analyst also did something
taboo, can last only as long as the analyst keeps doing this and, as in
hypnosis, as long as the rapport remains unclouded. *By no means* is such
an "interpretation" an interpretation in the true analytic sense, which is
a real confrontation of the experiencing ego with something which it had
previously warded off [pp. 45-46].[5]

Fenichel seems to be describing very nearly the process we have
been discussing throughout these last two chapters. His criterion,
however, for what is a "too deep interpretation" is after the fact
—that is, "when the patient cannot recognize its correctness by
experiencing the impulse in question." Recognizing the correctness of an interpretation by "experiencing the impulse in question" is an acceptable description of the feeling of anxiety
reduction that follows an accurately empathic response. However,
the therapist cannot wait to see what the client's response will be
to decide how to respond in the first place.

[5]From Fenichel, O. Problems of psychoanalytic technique. Albany, New York:
Psychoanalytic Quarterly, 1941. Reprinted by permission.

7

Adjunctive techniques and special problems

The preceding chapters have indicated that working in the conflict region is the central process by which therapeutic growth occurs. However, leadingly empathic responses are certainly not all that a therapist emits. For example, he must provide relatively constant levels of empathy for all kinds of messages from his client. And other behaviors that do not readily fit within our theoretical model are also necessary for the establishment of the therapeutic relationship and for "setting the stage" for therapeutic growth. The main focus of this chapter is on some of these other behaviors, and on the issue of specifying the content of therapy.

The content issue

In contrast to many psychoanalytic writers, who discuss much about the content of therapy and little about technique, I have tended to stress technique and perhaps to neglect content. What topics do the client and therapist talk about? Neglect of this issue has been partly intentional, since it is my conviction that, although there are certainly common themes among groups of clients, each client's specific set of conflicts is complicated and unique to him, and the therapist's task is to understand his client's uniqueness with great precision.

The answer to the question "What is the content of therapy?" is, then, that the content is unique for every client. There are common variables in the content of human problems, and the therapist must be knowledgeable enough to know these common variables; but he must also follow his client through the client's exploration of himself. Only the client can provide the precisely unique content that he is.

Personality theories.   Expert knowledge and a broad insightful grasp of the nature of the human condition can enable a therapist to hear his client sooner and with greater accuracy than a psychologically naive therapist might. Expert knowledge of the nature of personality and psychopathology, however, is still at a crude level, and no single theory of personality provides us with information that is precisely applicable to any individual person. Our theories are all incomplete and almost certainly incorrect to some degree. A flexible, healthy therapist can use his knowledge of personality and personality theories to enhance his ability to hear the precise nature of his client's experience; but if the therapist is emotionally committed to one or two particular theories, he is in considerable danger of fitting all of his clients to his theory, whether they fit or not. He is in danger of creating a self-fulfilling prophecy by hearing and reinforcing primarily what he wants to hear.

Personality tests.   The issue of personality tests is similar to the issue of personality theories. Tests can occasionally, if used judiciously, enhance the therapist's ability to hear a client's message earlier than he might otherwise have heard it. But because of the considerable lack of precision of the tests available, test information can also attune the therapist to a distorted view of what the client might be trying to say. As with personality theories, even accurate information from a personality test can be misused if it causes the therapist to respond beyond the conflict region, if it permits him to "see too much" and he is not then wise enough to wait until the client tries to approach the material that the therapist has already seen.

Our personality tests are too imprecise to provide us with unique meanings for any particular client, but they probably do serve a useful purpose in making gross diagnoses for the purpose of assigning a particular client to a particular therapist or particular kind of treatment. Some available evidence seems to indicate that psychological diagnosis can be made reliably within four broad categories: thought disorders (psychoses), neurosis, psychopathy, and organic disorders (Kreitman, 1961; Sandifer, Pettus, & Quade, 1964). This information is probably of some use in deciding, for example, that a disorder that is primarily organic would be more appropriately treated by retraining or by medical procedures than by anxiety-reducing therapy such as we are discussing. Even at this gross level, however, the information that a person is, say, displaying psychopathic behavior does not tell us whether the etiology of his problem is a lack of anxiety or too much anxiety, and any treatment decision we might make could be entirely reversed depending upon the etiology question. In addition, as we will see in the next chapter, describing a problem as neurotic is not a sufficiently precise judgment to decide whether the most appropriate treatment would be empathy-oriented therapy or some behavior-modification technique.

From outside the client's frame of reference

The therapist's main job is to hear his client and to communicate his understanding and acceptance—that is, to respond from within the client's frame of reference. There are many things, though, that a therapist must provide from his own frame of reference, and these are appropriate as long as the therapist remembers his main task. He occasionally and briefly responds from outside the client's frame of reference but continuously returns to the task of understanding.

Setting limits. Limits in psychotherapy provide the therapist with the knowledge that he can give of himself energetically and freely, knowing that too much cannot be demanded of him because of the limits that have been set. Many limits are already understood by the client when he comes to therapy: he knows that therapy has a specific time limit for each session, that he may not harm the therapist physically, and that the therapy relationship is essentially a one-way relationship of a very special nature. Some clients, however, are not clear about the existence of these limits, and many clients attempt to test and/or stretch the limits by, for example, asking that the therapy hour be extended, attempting to change the relationship into a social one outside of therapy, and perhaps subtly or overtly asking for physical affection from the therapist. In such instances, and in any case where a behavior violates the therapist's limits, he must take the responsibility for prohibiting that behavior. He should set the limit empathically, by expressing an understanding of the client's wishes and by stating the truth that the limit is established primarily for the therapist's sake.

Structuring and requests for advice.   Clients often enter therapy confused and uncertain about what is expected of them, and sometimes the therapist must provide a general statement about "how to do therapy." Therapy begins differently with each client, and many clients simply begin talking, perhaps in response to an expectant silence or gesture on the therapist's part. For other clients, however, most therapists provide some kind of an opening line that is appropriate to the situation. The therapist might say, for example, "Why don't you just talk about whatever is on your mind now?" or "I don't know very much about you, why don't you talk about whatever seems important?"

The therapist's job is to facilitate a process of mutual exploring, and he usually teaches this process to the client through his own behavior. Once the client begins talking, the therapist provides consistent understanding and acceptance, and he demonstrates, again through his behavior, that he can be trusted emotionally. Frequently, however, this procedure puzzles clients who have come to the therapist expecting advice very quickly, or who may engage in verbal exploration for a time and then have the expectation that, now that the "expert therapist" has some information, he can tell the client what to do. Even if the client were emotionally free to make use of good advice, only gods and advice columnists possess the wisdom to give specific direction for the solution of emotional problems on the basis of limited information. The therapist may have to teach the client how to do therapy by saying quite frankly that he feels unable to give such advice in a useful way. The therapist needs to go beyond this negative statement, however, since to the client the statement "I can't give you advice" may sound like "I don't know how I can help you." The therapist can express his own confidence in himself, describe the therapy process, communicate to the client his commitment and interest in helping the client solve his problems, and empathize with the client's desire for advice by some statement such as "It would be great if I could tell you exactly what to do; you could go out and do it and the problem would be solved. That would feel good and I can understand your wanting me to give you that kind of advice. I don't think I'm wise enough, though, to tell you exactly what to do and to tell you just how to live your life. I think there are things that neither of us understands yet about your problems. It has been my experience that the most effective way to deal with problems like this is for you to talk about your problems and feelings and explore what they mean, and my job is to help you do that exploring." Each therapist will of course make his own statement in his own words, and this kind of structuring should be used judiciously and relatively infrequently. It is often a mistake, however, to permit a client to wallow in his own confusion if the problem is that he simply doesn't know how to go about doing therapy. Discussion and evidence on this point can be found in Brammer and Shostrom (1968), Bierman (1969), and Truax and Carkhuff (1967).

Teaching.   Unlike Dollard and Miller, I do not see the therapist primarily as a teacher. The problem is not the client's lack of information but his inability to use the information that should be available to him from his own thought processes or from his environmental experiences. The therapist's task is to enable him to use such information but not necessarily to provide that information. In most cases, as the client becomes emotionally freer, he will be able to learn new adjustments for himself from his environmental experiences. There are, however, some circumstances in which the successful client has acquired an increased ability to use information that previously made him unbearably anxious but has not had the opportunity to acquire that information. It seems likely, for example, that there are some lessons about heterosexual behavior that society deems appropriate for an adolescent to learn but inappropriate for a 30-year-old. If a 30-year-old client passed through adolescence totally unable to deal with heterosexual relationships and now has resolved his conflicts, he may need information about himself in relation to other people. It may be appropriate for the therapist to provide this information, *providing* that a lack of information is really the problem. The obvious difficulty is that it is often hard to know when the problem is only a lack of information. There are dangers in becoming the client's advice-giving teacher, and the presence of these dangers demands that the therapist fill the teacher role, if at all, very seldom and judiciously. One goal of therapy is to increase the client's problem-solving ability. Having the therapist solve the client's problems, as opposed to only providing information, might well help the client out of one situation but teach him little about his own problem-solving abilities, and it may increase dependency upon the therapist and others in general for the solution of problems. An additional danger is that the therapist may misjudge the client's "ignorance" as a lack of information when the problem is still a conflict-laden anxiety problem, leading the client to see the therapist as a source of anxiety and as one who "doesn't understand." One additional danger is that the therapist may delude himself that he is giving information when he is really giving advice.

Effective therapy frees the client to learn from his experiences and mistakes. The therapist who gives advice will give both good and bad advice but more importantly will prevent the client's developing better problem-solving skills. However, a difficult problem exists when a client is about to do something that the therapist strongly believes will have serious long-term consequences that the client does not see. Direct advice or intervention may prevent disaster, but the therapist must weigh this against the client's increased dependency on him, against the implication that the therapist does not trust the client's judgment, and against the client's missed opportunity to learn from his own experience. Weighing all these factors demands a "judgment call" from the therapist, with serious consequences for a bad decision. In extreme examples the decision is clear—no competent therapist would permit a serious suicide attempt. As the decision enters gray areas, though, it is seldom clear and usually is best made in consultation with a colleague. Direct advice or intervention costs the therapist effectiveness as a reducer of internalized conflicts. Each such intervention must be weighed against its consequences.

Questioning. A brief comment on therapist questioning is of interest because beginning therapists tend to ask questions and experienced therapists tend to make declarative responses (Ornston,

Cicchetti, Levine, & Fierman, 1968). These tendencies are probably due partly to the novice therapist's inability to know what to say and his desire to keep the discussion going, often leading to a Perry Mason style of information-gathering and analysis in therapy. The repeated use of information-gathering questions creates the "set" for the client that therapy is an information-oriented process. Therapy is a mutual exploring process, and although questions are occasionally very appropriate, the therapist's main task is to facilitate exploration of thoughts and feelings through his empathic responses. Occasionally a leadingly empathic response is best formulated as a question, especially when the therapist is not quite sure he has heard the message. He might, for example, preface his response by asking "I'm not sure this is what you're saying, but is it that you . . . ?" By phrasing the response as a question the therapist has left the client freer to disagree with the response if he feels it did not capture the meaning of his message. A danger also exists, however, in the use of such empathic questions. The careless therapist can use what seem to be empathic questions to make interpretations based on his own formulation, although he tries to attribute the formulation to the client. He uses what is apparently an empathic attempt to ask a didactic, rhetorical question.

Client "overdoses"

My discussion of the theoretical model gave the impression that the client always approaches anxiety-provoking material in an orderly progression of small steps. This is nearly always the case, but occasionally a client will expose himself to a great deal of strongly anxiety-provoking material. This sometimes happens early in therapy because of the client's expectation that "one is supposed to tell one's therapist everything." Remember that exposure to anxiety-provoking cues is not sufficient; a strong counterconditioning agent must also be present. If the therapy relationship is not strong, exposure to embarrassing, anxiety-provoking material, even when initiated by the client, can cause therapy and the therapist to become anxiety cues and motivate the premature termination of therapy. The therapist must empathically sense whether the process the client is going through is one of dealing with difficult material and *continuously experiencing anxiety reduction* and relief (counterconditioning) in the presence of this difficult material. Dealing with highly emotionally charged material is often interesting and challenging for the therapist, but he must keep in mind that his job is to *continuously* reinforce the client's approach responses with continuous anxiety reduction in repeated small steps. If anxiety reduction does not follow the client's approach responses, he is being punished for his self-exploration, and the therapist can expect some kind of fleeing from therapy, perhaps through termination, perhaps through resistance, perhaps through a self-deceiving flight into health. When the client "overdoses" himself the therapist's task is to permit or sometimes even to help the client back off to the point where he can experience repeated anxiety reduction. This is especially true early in therapy. In the backing-off process the therapist does not intervene to prevent the discussion of material he deems too difficult; instead he responds empathically to the difficulty the client is having rather than to the content of what he is saying. The therapist might say "Some things are pretty hard to talk about" or "I guess it's difficult to plunge right into things with a person you don't know very well yet" or similar words that communicate an accurate understanding to the client.

Defensive clients

The approach to therapy we have been discussing depends on the client's producing responses to which the therapist can respond empathically. Sometimes, however, a therapist must deal with a silent client or with one who tends to externalize and defensively blame his environment and others for his condition, thereby producing very few self-exploratory responses. There is no question that these clients present great difficulty for all therapists and are frustrating to work with in therapy. The therapist's frustration often leads him to want to confront and directly attack the client's defenses, and some therapists recommend this technique for defensive clients (Reich, 1949; Ellis, 1962; Carkhuff & Berenson, 1967). However, I still would apply our theoretical model—although tentatively. Defensiveness has developed for such a client through the process of anxiety reduction and has to some extent been "successful." To the extent that his defenses are anxiety reducing, they have been strongly reinforced and can be given up only with great difficulty. An extensive research literature (Truax & Carkhuff, 1967) indicates that defensive clients often suggest a poor prognosis, regardless of the therapeutic approach. It may be that a therapist must face the fact that there is no fast way to deal with the extremely defensive client.

The dilemma a therapist faces is how to respond empathically to the client whose verbalizations seem primarily defensive. He might fear that empathic and accepting responses to defensive verbalizations will reinforce the client's defenses. To some extent that seems likely. On the other hand, by confronting and attacking the defenses, he is punishing the client's few self-exploratory responses and establishing himself as an aversive cue. Remember that if the client is in conflict *he will approach the elements of the conflict as much as he can stand to.* The therapist's job can be described as taking away the client's need for his defenses within the therapy hour by not being an anxiety arouser himself—by exhibiting his total understanding and acceptance without punishing the client for being defensive. Probably no client's verbalizations are entirely defensive; every client exhibits some self-exploration (if he doesn't, he is unlikely to have entered psychotherapy for neurotic problems). The therapist's job is to listen attentively and facilitate those attempts the client does make to explore himself. The therapist must realize that such a process is, with our present level of understanding, time consuming, slow, complicated, and often frustrating.

Clients with strongly felt disturbance and few overt symptoms make much more effective use of psychotherapy than do clients with less clearly felt disturbance and more overt symptoms (Truax & Carkhuff, 1967). At times therapy with a well-defended client will be time consuming and extended. If the therapist is unwilling or unable to make such a time commitment, an "economic" decision may have to be made, in which the client either receives no treatment so that others may use his treatment time or receives a more expedient kind of treatment with more limited goals than those we have set.

Carkhuff and Berenson (1967) call defensive clients "low-level functioning" clients and argue that therapy with these clients "must be on the therapist's terms" (p. 182). Direct guidance of the discussion, active intervention, and confrontation are recommended, and Carkhuff and Berenson offer some evidence that confrontation facilitates client self-exploration when it is offered by a therapist functioning at high levels of empathy, congruence, and positive regard. Pierce and Drasgow (1969) used these notions to study one-hour therapy sessions with three hospitalized veterans being treated for war injuries. During the session, each client-subject received 20 minutes of therapist responses described as "classical nondirective reflection"; 20 minutes of "conflict attention," which was defined as "going beyond reflection . . . by confronting the client with what he has not said between the lines, or what he has implied apart from the utilized content, or with any of the various implications of what he has said at deeper levels of meaning. If whatever we add amounts to focusing on a conflict, then we have 'conflict attention' " (p. 341); and finally, 20 minutes during which both reflection and conflict attention were "withheld." Client self-exploration was greatest during the segment of conflict attention, next greatest following reflection, and least during the period of withholding. These results are not surprising, if I correctly understand the difference between "classical nondirective reflection" and "conflict attention" as Pierce and Drasgow use the terms. Passive reflection should result in virtually no therapeutic gains if used alone. Clearly more is needed. In our attempts to grope for what that "more" is, others and I may be using different words for the same phenomena, so I would like to try to translate "confrontation" and "conflict attention" into the terms of my theoretical model—at the risk of exposing a misunderstanding of Carkhuff and Berenson, who seem to mean more than "leading empathy" when they talk about confrontation.

Pierce and Drasgow suggest that "the *sine qua non* of good therapy and counseling now may have to shift from reflection to conflict attention in order to speed up client self-exploration . . . A deeper meaning of the shift from reflective to conflict attention threatens a much greater alteration in our therapeutic posture. It signals changing from a passive reflective role to an *active* aggressive one. It means we should lead the client rather than follow him, and as such the attention to conflict puts more responsibility and all that it implies on us" (p. 342). This description of the "something more" could easily be confused with interpretation—which has been discussed for years. My guess is that I might function as a therapist in a way similar to Pierce and Drasgow, but I think that conflict attention can be most usefully and clearly thought of as deeply exploring empathy. The focus is on an attempt to understand what the client is struggling to understand—which is a different approach from the therapist's seeing himself as the source of new knowledge and new implications in the client's words. There is no question that the therapist must be an active participant, but "active" must not be confused with attacking, controlling, or aggressing. He must be actively empathic, struggling to grasp the nuances of his client's inner world, listening attentively for the painful edges of the client's message, focusing his energy on the client and his attempts to explore himself.

Carkhuff and Berenson's approach to confrontation does not fit so neatly within my model of therapy. They seem to say that a client functioning at a high level (less defensive, more able to explore verbally) can best be treated by a therapist who "focuses on the crises and resolution of crises through full confrontation" (p. 190). Here their discussion of confrontation seems to me similar to what I would call leading empathy or exploring empathy. However, they clearly mean something different by confrontation when discussing the client who is functioning at a low level. Their descriptions and examples suggest a direct attack on the client's defenses, with therapist interventions such as "Right now shut up Stan!— and you listen to me (reaches over and shakes the client by the shoulders and shouts) Damn! You think too much—listen!" (p. 183). This approach resembles the psychoanalysts' attack on the defenses and seems clearly inconsistent with my model. I suspect that such an attack might in some cases increase the client's attention to therapy, make him work harder, and more strongly convince him that the therapist is truly interested in him. These gains are won at a price, however, and that price *may* not have to be paid if the therapist can afford the longer time to facilitate self-exploration and help the client toward greater independence. The question is an empirical one. If we can agree on different definitions for confrontation and leading empathy, their effects can be tested with defensive clients.

The length of therapy

Whether therapy is to be of short or long term depends on the severity and complexity of the client's conflicts. Only a few sessions might be sufficient for mild problems, while severely anxiety-arousing, multifaceted conflicts will require many sessions.

That is, relatively mild conflicts can be resolved by the counter-conditioning effects of a briefly established relationship, while powerfully anxiety-arousing conflicts would require the establishment of a powerful counterconditioner and many counterconditioning experiences.

My model portrays therapy as a *continuously progressing* relief of conflicts. A correct implication of this view is that some therapy is better than none, even though the client's problems may be far from solved. Therapy is not a process that, once started, must be completed; it is not an opening of emotional wounds that must be entirely healed lest the client leave therapy bleeding. Anxiety-arousing material is exposed only to the extent that it can be dealt with at the moment—in the process of exposing it.

Termination, even of "incomplete" therapy, should leave the client less conflicted and better able to deal with his problems. An exception to this probably exists in those cases in which a strong transference has developed. Resolution of such a problem probably requires the maintenance of the therapy relationship until the resolution is completed.

Termination

Our theoretical model provides little help in deciding when and how therapy is to be terminated. Certainly the model applies to any attempt on the client's part to discuss termination. The therapist's job, as it is with other topics, is to hear what the client is trying to say and help him say it, and this is certainly the most desirable and usual termination procedure. The process of therapy as we have outlined it, however, is potentially endless. Every person suffers from some conflicts and every person is to some extent neurotic. To this extent each of us could benefit from a therapy relationship or, as is hopefully the case for each of us, some other kind of relationship with therapeutic qualities. There are limits, however, that both therapists and society place on the appropriate application of formal psychotherapy. In most cases, therapy is initiated because of pain or unsatisfactory life circumstances; the pain is intense enough to justify the effort and cost of seeking psychotherapy. Presumably as the pain diminishes a point is reached at which the cost and effort are greater than the need. The time at which this point occurs is extremely difficult to specify. The therapist's fee may be nothing to the wealthy client and everything to the poor client. Free therapy at a clinic might be continued by a client who no longer is suffering more than "normal" because he sees it as enhancing the quality of his life. His continued therapy, however, is being paid for by someone—perhaps the clinic, perhaps society—and in addition, the therapist's time that is being devoted to this client might more productively be devoted to a more seriously disturbed client. The therapist, in other words, is forced sometimes to make economic decisions about his own limits and the termination of therapy. A dilemma is posed, however, since the initiation of termination by the therapist almost always bears some message of rejection of the client, at least in the client's eyes. Interestingly, some evidence (Phillips & Johnston, 1954; Shlien, Mosak, & Dreikurs, 1962) indicates that the establishment of real time limits such as the client's ending a school term or leaving town for external reasons may facilitate the therapy process and provide a termination that does not involve the therapist's "rejection" of the client.

Group therapy

A recent trend in the therapy field has been toward group treatment. It has been argued that individual therapy is simply too expensive, in terms of both money and therapist time. Many have also argued that group treatment is often more efficacious than individual treatment, because of the nature of particular problems as well as the nature of groups.

Although I will not deal with group therapy in detail, the theoretical model is clearly applicable to the group situation. The principles of neurosis and treatment are the same; the alleviation of intrapersonal conflicts still depends on the client's responses being met by understanding and acceptance. One of the advantages of therapy conducted in a group is that the members of the group can each act as therapists. Often as group therapy progresses the members of the group begin to treat each other in the manner they have learned from the therapist. If the therapist is consistently empathic and accepting, the members of the group tend to learn to respond in a similar way to other members of the group. Obviously, the great advantage is that acceptance from six people is stronger and generalizes more broadly to experience outside of therapy.

The potential of group psychotherapy is great, especially for clients whose problems are primarily interpersonal. Dangers exist, however, in group treatment—mainly because the therapist has less control over each client's receiving understanding and acceptance. If interpreting and attacking an individual client beyond the conflict region is damaging, the same damage can be done by a group, and the group therapist must be alert to and deal wisely with such attacks between group members. The recent popularity of encounter groups has occasionally led to the notion that encounter means attack. As in individual therapy, an encounter with empathic, accepting people who are really themselves in the relationship is therapeutic. The key issue is that the encounter takes place in the context of empathy and acceptance and not in the context of attack and exposure.

This chapter could have been called "Miscellaneous" or "Other Thoughts I've Had." It has been a brief attempt to deal with the problems of functioning in the real world as a therapist, and it could go on much longer. In general, I have tried to show how some problems do not fit the theoretical model but can be dealt with in a way not inconsistent with the model—or how their solution can be sought within the perspective of the model.

I consider the issue of confronting defensive clients to be an unresolved one, and I am not ready to resolve it in this book. But in the future I will try to resolve it within the limits of the model, since that seems at present to be the most productive approach. If evidence contradicts my thinking, I will have to expand the model or perhaps limit its applicability even more than I have.

I have already limited the model within the last few years in the attempt to specify the conditions under which behavior modification is appropriate. This attempt has taken on considerable importance in my thinking, so I have treated it separately in the next chapter. It could have been discussed in this chapter, though, since what I have tried to do here is show how the model can be used as a structure within which many problems can be thought through.

8

Using behavior modification

Although the principles by which interview therapy works are the same as those underlying behavior modification, interview-oriented therapists and behavior modifiers generally look askance at each other. I agree with Bandura's comment that "Much time has been spent fruitlessly in attempts to define what constitutes 'behavior therapy' and 'psychotherapy.' A more productive and less confusing approach to the understanding of social-influence processes is to focus on the basic mechanisms through which behavioral changes are produced" (1969, p. 463). The differences between empathy-oriented therapy and behavior modification lie in the *application* of the principles, and I will try to integrate the two techniques and specify when each is appropriate.

I have argued that neurotic problems involving internalized conflicts are most effectively treated in empathy-oriented psychotherapy. Therapy based on the conflict model seems most effective for the relief of the four major neurotic problems: maladaptive anxiety-reducing behaviors, anxiety experiences, inadequate problem-solving ability, and painfully low self-esteem. For reasons of economy a therapist and a client may sometimes have to settle for less than the alleviation of all four general problems. Extended psychotherapy may be called for but unavailable, and the removal of specific symptoms may be all that is possible under certain circumstances. In addition to such an economic decision, however, some neurotic problems are most effectively treated through behavior-modification techniques. It is also likely that much psychopathic behavior will yield only to some kind of clearly specified and strongly applied retraining procedures.

Defining exactly what techniques are and are not behavior modification is becoming increasingly difficult, since new techniques are proliferating so fast, including "total behavioral management" (Franks, 1969) and "technical eclecticism" (Lazarus, 1967). There is no list of techniques to which behavior modifiers subscribe. Rather, the emphasis is on principles of learning, and specific techniques are limited only by the imaginative application of the principles to the complexities of individual cases. Using this broad definition, one student has argued that I am a behavior modifier —which is in a sense true, since the principles of my model are explicitly learning-based. Also, the process of empathy-based therapy can be seen as a form of graduated counterconditioning or systematic desensitization. Again the principles are the same; the differences lie in the application of the principles. The distinctions between psychotherapy and behavior modification seem artificial and misleading when seen in this light.

For the purposes of this chapter, however, I will maintain the distinction by specifying the conditions appropriate for therapist-controlled direct modification of overt behavior, using techniques within three general classes: desensitization, aversive counterconditioning, and positive reinforcement.

Directly conditioned fears

Chapter 3 differentiated directly conditioned fears from anxiety, which is based on conflict. An example was cited in which a colleague treated a directly conditioned fear of dogs with the behavior-modification technique of pairing the presence of dogs with pleasant stimuli. This case is very similar to the classic case reported by Mary Cover Jones (1924), in which she alleviated a little boy's fear of rabbits through a progressively closer presentation of a rabbit while the boy was experiencing pleasant stimuli such as eating ice cream. This appropriate application of a behavior-modification technique should be contrasted with a potential treatment of the hypothetical case developed in Chapter 3. A second boy also feared dogs—but in the truly phobic sense; that is, his fear was anxiety reducing. The real fear cue was not dogs; it involved an intense conflict over his mother's actions and his fear of his own dependency impulses. The etiology of his fear was based on an internalized conflict. Directly reconditioning his fear of dogs would be an inappropriate treatment unless, at the same time, his internalized conflict was resolved.

It is relevant that much of the laboratory research reported by behavior modifiers has to do with the alleviation of fears of snakes, rats, and spiders. These fears are almost certainly directly conditioned fears, based on social and imitative learning, and they are sometimes debilitating. Intense fear of snakes, for example, might prevent the enjoyment of camping and picnics, or it might even prevent one's leaving the house when harmless snakes might be encountered. Direct reconditioning of such fears seems a most appropriate treatment, but a serious question must be raised about the analogy drawn between the fear of snakes, rats, and spiders and the internalized conflicts associated with neurotic problems. Recall my criticisms of behavior modification in Chapter 2, where I discussed the apparently oversimplified view of neurosis presented by many proponents of this position.

Externalized conflict

Chapter 3 drew a somewhat arbitrary distinction between internalized conflict, in which the individual's motivated impulses have become fear cues, and externalized conflict, in which the individual has both approach and avoidance tendencies for some object outside himself. The distinction is arbitrary because externalized conflict obviously involves some internal cues, since the individual is thinking about the object, and his approach tendencies thus involve internal impulses. In addition, nearly all individuals' conflicts are combinations of internalized and externalized conflicts. However, the distinction does have some practical applications if we think of externalized conflicts as those based *primarily* on external cues and internalized conflicts as those cued by motivated impulses. Externalized conflicts might well be treated by direct reconditioning procedures.

An example of this kind of approach is represented by the excellent series of studies reported by Gordon Paul (1966, 1967), in which he reported the use of reciprocal-inhibition techniques for the treatment of stage fright. He successfully treated, and followed up over a long period of time, college students who were unable to present speeches in front of a class. An oversimplified analysis of stage fright, in terms of conflict, might see its cause as an approach tendency based on a desire to pass the course and an avoidance tendency based on the fear of other people's judgments. The elements of the conflict might be seen as primarily external and not based on fear of the individual's internally motivated impulses. Several appropriate reconditioning procedures might be undertaken to reduce the individual's fear of the presence of other individuals. He might, for example, be strongly rewarded after presenting a speech to one nonthreatening person. He might then move through his "anxiety hierarchy" by being strongly rewarded for presenting a speech to two people. Presumably this procedure would eventually recondition him by reducing his fear response to the presence of other people. By the same token, systematic desensitization using imagined fear situations could also have some effect in reducing the power of an audience as a fear cue, as it seemed to be in Paul's studies. It is also interesting that "insight therapy" was somewhat effective in improving the performance of one of Paul's control groups. This may have been due to the fact that relearning occurred in the "insight group" and possibly to the fact that the subjects' stage fright was also partly based on internalized conflicts.

If a client's conflicts are based on external cues and those cues can be accurately ascertained (stringent conditions), then direct reconditioning of the fear response to the external cues is an entirely appropriate therapeutic approach.

Nonadaptive habits based on former conflicts

Conceivably a self-defeating behavior pattern might develop through the process of anxiety reduction and be so strongly reinforced that at a later time, even though the original conflict may have been resolved, the well-reinforced behavior might survive. Since this behavior is somehow punishing (otherwise it's not neurotic), the usual fate of such behaviors is that they are punished out of existence by interaction with the environment. Since they are no longer necessary for the avoidance of the now resolved conflict, they are no longer the lesser of two pains, and the laws of reinforcement would work to eliminate the behavior. (This is almost certainly one process by which "spontaneous cures" occur.) However, some maladaptive behaviors such as excessive smoking and drinking are self-perpetuating in that, even when they are no longer needed as anxiety reducers, physiological needs may prevent their elimination. In addition and more subtly, the establishment of an anxiety-reducing behavior pattern may prevent the learning of other patterns even when the anxiety-reducing function is no longer needed. Or a deviant behavior, such as fetishism, may be repeatedly and strongly reinforced by sexual pleasure, establishing the behavior so strongly that new learning is precluded. If it can be established that a neurotic problem has such an etiology and that it no longer serves an anxiety-reducing function, symptom removal by any means practical is called for.

The most commonly used approach to the modification of maladaptive behaviors being maintained by positive reinforcement is aversion therapy. Pairing the undesired stimuli with pain presumably reduces their power as reinforcers. The use of emetics in alcohol and shock presented with homosexual or fetishistic images are examples of such attempts. The success of these procedures has been very mixed and seems to depend on whether or not concomitant techniques are used. Aversion therapy alone is relatively unsuccessful and may even intensify problems, such as drinking, by arousing even greater anxiety, for which further drinking serves as an anxiety reducer (Menaker, 1967). Aversion therapy used with some program of positive reinforcement, however, can be designed to both eliminate the undesirable behavior and establish a new and more desirable behavior pattern. Unfortunately, programs of positive reinforcement in real life must be extremely complex to be of any real use to a client. The complexities are so overwhelming that a therapist might be tempted to fall back on bromides and simplified "rules for living." The effective use of aversion treatment probably demands that it be used in conjunction with the problem-solving focus of empathy-oriented therapy. It should be viewed as an adjunct to therapy.

An illustration of the complexities and pitfalls of naive applications of aversion therapy can be seen in the treatment of overweight. To a large extent, eating is obviously maintained by positive reinforcement, and some behavior modifiers (Cautela, 1969) have paired aversive stimuli with food as a treatment of overweight. This approach should work with cases where overeating is maintained only by positive reinforcement; for many individuals, for example, the punishments of overweight are distant, and the reinforcement of eating is immediate. An eclair today is more powerful than a heart attack in thirty years. At some point, the punishments of being overweight become more powerful than the rewards of eating and the individual slows his eating before becoming grossly overweight. Often, however, overeating is maintained in a truly neurotic way; it can be anxiety reducing to be fat—in as many different ways as there are fat people. Overweight can punish an unconsciously hated spouse or parent by embarrassing them; although self-destructive, overeating is maintained by the reduction of the hatred-based conflict. Overweight can force social withdrawal and prevent being asked on dates, relieving the pain of social anxiety. The illustrations could go on forever, but the principle should be clear. Aversion treatment of food would be naive in such cases unless it were used only as a minor adjunct to the treatment of the underlying conflict; food isn't particularly reinforcing—being fat is. Many overeaters consistently gorge to the point of becoming nauseated—often on undesirable food; such behavior is sort of a naturalistic aversion treatment that doesn't work.

Aversion therapy also requires an unusual level of cooperation from the client, since the treatment is painful and he is being deprived of a source of pleasure. This is probably another reason why eliminating undesirable behaviors through aversion therapy demands that a rewarding and positive treatment approach be provided at the same time.

Debilitating behaviors and very specific fears

Although empathy-oriented interview therapy seems most effective in dealing with internalized conflicts, this treatment format makes a number of demands on clients. Inability to talk because of anxiety or refusal to leave home, for example, would preclude any kind of interview, regardless of whether the problem involved internalized conflicts. An innovative application of behavior-modification techniques might serve as a preliminary step to interview therapy in such a case.

If a highly specific fear can be identified, its quick relief through desensitization can be motivating and rewarding even though internalized conflicts underlie the fear. This quick success, however, should be seen only as a preliminary step to therapy and should be presented to the client in that light. If the fear was a directly conditioned fear, therapy would, of course, appropriately be over when the fear was relieved. But a potentially destructive possibility is that the relief of a specific fear that is not a directly conditioned one will also be seen as the end of therapy and turn out to be a temporary gain to be followed by distressing setbacks and the feeling that "even therapy didn't work for me."

The importance of "diagnostic" understanding

In specifying the conditions under which direct behavior-modification techniques are appropriate, decisions must be based on the presence or absence of internalized conflict and the importance of internalized conflict in the maintenance of the neurotic problem. Deciding whether such conditions are met requires a clear understanding of the etiology of each client's unique problems, but—to repeat—the early understandings of both the client and therapist are doomed to be at least partially incorrect. In a few cases, such as the boy who was badly bitten by a dog, the etiology of the problem will be relatively clear. In most neurotic problems, however, accurately establishing the etiology of a problem will require extensive verbal exploration of the nature of the problem. Where distortions are involved, the process of empathy-oriented therapy I have been describing seems the most efficient and accurate way of developing an understanding of the client's problems. Therapy requires a continually emerging and changing understanding by both the client and the therapist. To this extent, it is a "diagnostic" problem, although the effective therapist does not approach his task as that of diagnosing his client. In fact, the emerging understanding of the client's problems occurs as a by-product of therapeutic growth.

The importance of such diagnostic understanding is perhaps most clearly seen in the treatment of children. The classic understanding of school phobia, for example, is that the school-phobic child is not truly afraid of school but rather is afraid of leaving his mother, perhaps for fear his mother will be gone when he gets back, perhaps because he may lose mother's affection to a sibling, or for any of a number of reasons. Such a fear of school would be truly phobic in the sense that it is an anxiety-reducing fear. Other children, however, might fear school because of painful experiences at school. Assuming that these painful experiences are no longer occurring, a process of direct reconditioning of school as a fear cue would be an appropriate treatment. In the former case, however, effective treatment would have to be centered around the child's conflicts over his relationship with his mother. The therapist's task requires the accurate identification of the stimuli of the relevant emotional behavior. To apply behavior modification, Bandura (1969) has recommended "new assessment procedures ... for isolating stimulus determinants. ... Because of the countless and complex varieties of learning histories represented by clinic populations, a highly flexible stimulus exploration procedure is required" (p. 463). I would argue that the most efficient stimulus-exploration procedure follows the therapist's accurate empathy, and, further, *therapeutic progress and stimulus exploration occur simultaneously.*

Combining approaches

The flexible therapist should be attentive to the fact that behavior-modification techniques might be appropriate in therapy, under much the same conditions as those for the therapist filling the role of teacher. Many of the dangers of the teacher role also apply to the role of the therapist as behavior modifier, since much depends on the accuracy of the judgment that a particular problem is not based on internalized conflicts. A possibility also exists that the therapist will be casting himself in the role of the expert healer rather than contributing to the client's ability to solve his own problems.

With these cautions in mind, a therapist might well incorporate behavior-modification techniques into interview therapy. For example, a specific fear may be obviously based on direct conditioning or on a former conflict that still involves conditioned reactions because of a lack of opportunity for relearning. The therapist could use behavioral techniques to modify such specific fears, although the emphasis in therapy would continue to be on self-exploration. The principles of therapeutic progress are the same for both approaches. They differ only in application, and a competent therapist should be familiar with different means of applying the basic principles.

A recent case study by Naar (1970) reports the "peaceful coexistence" of client-centered therapy and behavior modification and illustrates many of the issues discussed in this chapter.[1] Naar argues that many observers have noted a trend toward cross-fertilization among approaches to psychotherapy and between traditional therapy approaches and more scientific psychology. Although this growing rapprochement seems desirable to him, he points out that there is a major stumbling block to the actual application of both approaches by individual therapists—a stumbling block I personally have had difficulty with. The philosophical orientation of the client-centered therapist is that man is to be free to choose the direction of his life and that he is truly capable of doing so. The behavior modifier implicitly assumes that it is his responsibility to plan and direct the course of therapy, which should not be "left to the vagaries of clients" but should be "carefully regulated by psychotherapists" (Bandura, 1969, p. 484). Naar's solution to this philosophical conflict has been to present the possibility of specific behavior-modification techniques as available at the client's option. The attractiveness of the techniques would undoubtedly depend largely on the way the therapist presented them, but Naar has presented the alternatives and limits of the approach as objectively as possible.

The client Naar discusses is a woman with incapacitating phobic symptoms, which began after serious anxiety attacks. She was unable to travel on buses, cars, and elevators and was unable to bear being left alone. The first phase of therapy was a combination

---

[1]D'Alessio (1968) has also described his attempts to combine behavior-modification techniques with a general psychoanalytic approach.

of client-centered therapy and systematic desensitization aimed at the specific fears that prevented her travel. After four months of treatment she was capable of greater mobility than she had ever been, but she still had a high level of generalized anxiety. During the second phase of treatment, empathy-based therapy was used to help her recognize and express her feelings, which turned out to be related to severe conflicts over the expression of anger. A third phase of therapy was begun when an unexpected pregnancy seemed to cause a relapse of the progress made. This phase was also client-centered therapy, which helped prepare the client for what turned out to be a tragic situation: the baby died shortly after birth.

Naar presents an interesting behavioral analysis of the dynamics of this case; his discussion is consistent with the presentation in this book, except that I would have placed more emphasis on the fact that his client's problems were based on internalized conflicts over anger. The appropriate relief of these conflicts required empathy-based therapy, and the simple removal of symptoms would have been an inappropriate treatment. As Naar points out, though, treatment with client-centered therapy alone would also have been inappropriate, since her phobic fears were so crippling that she could not or would not have been amenable to such treatment. Systematic desensitization made her capable of empathy-based therapy and gave her the satisfaction of concrete and quick progress.

Polemics and hostility between more traditional psychotherapists and behavior modifiers have been elicited and emitted by both sides, and the resultant split has hampered communication among therapists. Both groups have distorted the other's positions, and we must hope that we will move toward integration and winnowing of ideas, rather than toward the kind of rigidification of "schools" that has marked psychotherapy in the past.

9

On being eclectic

I have been trying to specify ways to be systematically eclectic—
to draw from the contributions of different approaches under
different circumstances and to be able to specify those circumstances. The noble goal of being systematically eclectic is an impossible dream, though, and I have no illusions that my thinking
and practice are unbiased by my personal needs, my distortions,
and my areas of ignorance. Brammer and Shostrom (1968) have
discussed the stages a developing therapist goes through as (1) the
general level, in which he is heavily influenced by his teachers,
whose ideas are incorporated within the context of the student's
own personal background, (2) the personalized level, in which the
influences of his personality modify his training experiences, (3)
the stylized level, in which he forms a commitment to certain
approaches that develop into a general style of functioning, and
(4) the expressive level, at which a few practitioners share the
unique parameters of their personal style with colleagues. Our
concern in this chapter is with the questions of commitment to a

position, the influence of personal factors, and the effects these variables have on creative thinking and progress in the area of developing new approaches to therapy.[1] Commitment seems necessary for effective functioning as a practitioner and even for motivating creative thinking, but unless the commitment is tempered by a willingness, or maybe even a desire, to change, new and contradictory thoughts and evidence will be so threatening that they will be rejected or ignored.

Dogmatism is the enemy of progress, especially in an area so complex and young that no one can possibly be entirely correct. Dogmatism has plagued therapy, however, and it seems to have stemmed from two general roots: (1) personal characteristics of theorists who cannot tolerate criticism and disagreement and who reject others' ideas summarily and (2) inadequacies in the state of our knowledge; our lack of evidence permits wildly differing interpretations of the same phenomena, with no way to distinguish which is the more parsimonious explanation; pseudo-differences arise out of semantic differences, which mask areas of true agreement; peripheral issues arise and consume debate as though they were central issues.

It seems unlikely that much can be done directly to make theorists personally more tolerant of change or to reduce their need for closure and certainty. We can only hope that relatively free individuals will be attracted to the development of new approaches to therapy. Rogers has commented (1963) that "The field of psychotherapy is in a mess. Therapists are not in agreement as to their goals or aims in therapy. They are in deep disagreement as to the theoretical structure which would contain their work" (p. 9). He bases his hope for the future of therapy on his belief:

that we are backing off and taking a fresh look at the basic problem of our profession, with no inhibitions, few preconceptions, and no holds barred. We can ask again the central question, "How may constructive change in the behavior and personality of the troubled or deviant person be facilitated?" Another implication is that for the time being it will be a young man's field. The curiosity and skepticism, the vigor and creativity of younger minds are freed by this chaotic situation. No longer is it governed by the heavy hand of supposedly wise elders. Young men are free to go at the problems freshly, without the sense of being rebels [p. 11].

[1]Several ideas in this chapter were contributed by Larry Hershfield.

Perhaps youth does free one from the commitments and possibly the rigidity that prevent new ideas. Maybe emotional health has more to do than age with creativity. Regardless, the therapist must somehow combine the qualities of tentative commitment, seeking change but not being too ready to accept change without compelling evidence and reason, being willing to meld from one position to another without rejecting all of the less tenable approaches. He must be eclectic in as systematic a way as he can without using the word "eclectic" to hide the fact that he doesn't know what he does or why. He must be able to stand the pain of exposing his ideas to the criticism of others and to modify rather than rigidify in the face of valid attack.

Changing the personal influences on the creative process would be an overwhelming task, but there are some formal ways to reduce the effects of the second influence on dogmatism—inadequacies in the state of our knowledge. Illusory differences are often based on fallacious semantic differences, and review of terminology can show areas where one position can be translated into the language of another. When this process of review reveals concepts that seem truly different in different approaches, an attempt should be made at integration. Can the concepts of one approach be explained in a more parsimonious way by a different approach? Can apparent inconsistencies in explanation by two views both be explained by a third approach—even though aspects of the third view are untenable? When integration reveals an irreconcilable impasse, the co-existence of incompatible ideas should be temporarily tolerated —if not within individuals, at least within the field. The most sensible strategy for both research and theory in the therapy field is to settle for continuously shifting approximations of what is most effective under specific conditions. We probably need more theories for many specific conditions, rather than one overall theory to account for all therapy phenomena.

Rogers (1963) has suggested that new knowledge in therapy will come primarily from three sources: naturalistic observation, empirical studies of actual therapy, and therapy-relevant research in the laboratory setting. Ideally, naturalistic observation would require therapists to immerse themselves in their own functioning in therapy and in observing the functioning of others, primarily by listening to tape recordings. This listening process should be approached in as nontheoretical a way as possible. Every therapist, of course, is bound by at least some form of low-level theory by which he organizes his experience, but he can gain from naturalistic observation if he can continuously ask himself "What seems to be working and why?" It is probably especially useful to listen receptively to others whose behaviors are inconsistent with one's own functioning and then to try to understand why those behaviors might be therapeutic. The conduct of empirical research on actual therapy has expanded fairly steadily since Rogers and Dymond (1954) published their pioneering work, but it has faced many problems and seems only now to be having much effect on the conduct of psychotherapy. Bergin (1966) outlined the implications of therapy research for practice, and others, such as Truax and Carkhuff (1967), have applied research on accurate empathy, congruence, and nonpossessive warmth to the training of therapists at both the professional and subprofessional levels, but the problems are still formidable. A good recent discussion can be found in Strupp and Bergin (1969). The use of laboratory analogues to therapy seems to be lessening, according to Strupp and Bergin, primarily because the information yielded by such studies seems to have been so distant from application in therapy that the influence of such studies has been even less than the influence of research on situations defined as actual therapy. Elsewhere (Martin, 1971) I have argued that the most sensible strategy for research in therapy demands successive approximations combining the best available process and outcome measures, with the understanding that critical studies are not possible at our level of sophistication of theory and methodology. As in the area of theory development, therapy research demands flux, synthesis, and integration.

The attitude and approach I have described are consistent with an increasing de-emphasis on schools of psychotherapy and a greater concern for the etiology of different kinds of problems and for specifying different approaches to different clearly defined problems. Both of these trends seem to be dominant in the current literature on therapy. Years ago Thorne (1957) made a strong plea for eclecticism, but only recently has an eclectic mood gained wide acceptance. The older pattern of aggressive rejection of whole theories is evident in some of the 'clashes between behavior modifiers and psychoanalysts, but hopefully this clash will yield to the more tolerant and flexible attitude that the therapy field needs. Kiesler (1966) noted that one of the myths of psychotherapy research is the "uniformity assumption"; therapy is often referred to as a unitary phenomenon and clients are treated as though their problems could be subsumed under one category; the statement "Those with emotional problems should be treated by psychotherapy" is meaningless. Paul has noted (1967) that the question "Does therapy work?" is just as meaningless:

Psychotherapy comprehends a most diversified set of procedures ranging from suggestion, hypnosis, reassurance, and verbal conditioning to systematic sets of actions and strategies based upon more or less tight theoretical formulations. . . . What is the appropriate question to be asked of outcome research? In all its complexity, the question toward which all outcome research should ultimately be directed is the following: *What* treatment, by *whom,* is most effective for *this* individual with *that* specific problem and under *which* set of circumstances? [p. 111.]

Kiesler (1969) has more recently expanded his thinking on specifying treatments for disorders and has suggested a "grid model" to be used for assigning specific client problems to specific therapists who use specific approaches. We clearly lack sufficient knowledge to apply Kiesler's grid model in applied situations, but his approach reflects the trend toward synthesis and integration of approaches.

Strupp and Bergin (1969) have made an exhaustive review of the state of research, and to some extent theory, in psychotherapy and have noted that "The barriers separating the major schools of psychotherapy are gradually being eroded, and the predominant direction of research is toward a nonschool approach" (p. 24). They cite many signs of an approaching rapprochement among learning approaches, client-centered approaches, and to some extent psychoanalysis, although they see "an increasing disaffection from psychoanalysis" (p. 31). This decline in schoolism has resulted in the training of therapists "becoming increasingly pragmatic and decreasingly theoretical. Therapists are expected to produce results, and students are being trained accordingly" (p. 30). I think that this emphasis on what works can bring both benefits and dangers. Broadening our repertoire of pragmatic behaviors in therapy will broaden the base of our naturalistic observation and lead to new insights and innovative treatment techniques. This atheoretical groping, however, needs the corrective influence of continuous justification in theoretical terms. An atheoretical shotgun approach is heavily dependent on the intuitive judgment and therefore the emotional health of the therapist. An honest therapist should be able to offer at least a tentative explanation for why what he does works, and he should be continuously checking whether it really does "work," in a way that is not subject to the distortions caused by his own needs.

Truax and Carkhuff (1967) have applied learning notions to the understanding of client-centered therapy in a somewhat different (but not inconsistent) manner from the way I have in this book. They called their effort a "tentative step toward a constructive encounter between the emerging behavior therapy and traditional conversation therapy" (p. 161). I have written this book as a further step in the same direction. It does not represent an attempt to establish a "new approach"; the field has become too mature (or maybe it's just too confused) to buy a new school. This book is a synthesis and integration of one small corner of a complicated problem. I hope it will be a helpful synthesis, but I reserve the right to alter my views in the face of new evidence and experiences.

References

Amsel, A. Hope comes to learning theory. *Contemporary Psychology,* 1961, *6*(2), 33–36.

Ashby, J. D., Ford, D. H., Guerney, B. G., Jr., & Guerney, L. F. Effects on clients of a reflective and leading type of psychotherapy. *Psychological Monographs: General and Applied,* 1957, *71*(24).

Bandura, A. *Principles of behavior modification.* New York: Holt, Rinehart and Winston, 1969.

Bandura, A. & Menlove, F. L. Factors determining vicarious extinction of avoidance behavior through symbolic modelling. *Journal of Personality and Social Psychology,* 1968, *8*(2), 99–108.

Beecroft, R. S. Near-goal punishment of avoidance running. *Psychonomic Science,* 1967, *8*(3), 109–110.

Beecroft, R. S. & Bouska, S. A. Learning self-punitive running. *Psychonomic Science,* 1967, *8*(3), 107–108.

Beecroft, R. S., Bouska, S. A. & Fisher, B. G. Punishment, intensity and self-punitive behaviour. *Psychonomic Science,* 1967, *8*(9), 351–352.

Beecroft, R. S. & Brown, J. S. Punishment following escape and avoidance training. *Psychonomic Science,* 1967, *8*(9), 349–350.

Berenson, B. G., Mitchell, K. M. & Laney, R. C. Level of therapist functioning types of confrontation and type of patient. *Journal of Clinical Psychology,* 1969, *25,* 111–113.

143

Bergin, A. E. The effects of psychotherapy: Negative results revisited. *Journal of Counseling Psychology,* 1963, *10,* 244–250.

Bergin, A. E. Some implications of psychotherapy research for therapeutic practice. *Journal of Abnormal Psychology,* 1966, *71,* 235–246.

Bergin, A. E. The deterioration effect: A reply to Braucht. *Journal of Abnormal Psychology,* 1970, *75*(3), 300–302.

Bierman, R. Dimensions of interpersonal facilitation in psychotherapy and child development. *Psychological Bulletin,* 1969, *72*(5), 338–352.

Braaten, L. J. The movement from non-self to self in client centered psychotherapy. Unpublished doctoral dissertation, University of Chicago, 1958.

Brammer, L. M. & Shostrom, E. L. *Therapeutic psychology: Fundamentals of actualization counselling and psychotherapy.* Englewood Cliffs, New Jersey: Prentice-Hall, 1968.

Braucht, G. N. The deterioration effect: A reply to Bergin. *Journal of Abnormal Psychology,* 1970, *75,* 293–299.

Breger, L. & McGaugh, J. L. Critique and reformulation of "learning theory" approaches to psychotherapy and neurosis. *Psychological Bulletin,* 1965, *63,* 338–358.

Brown, J. S. Gradients of approach and avoidance responses and their relation to level of motivation. *Journal of Comparative and Physiological Psychology,* 1948, *41,* 450–465.

Brown, J. S. Principles of intrapersonal conflict. *Conflict Resolution,* 1957, *1,* 135–154.

Brown, J. S. *The motivation of behavior.* New York: McGraw-Hill, 1961.

Brown, J. S. A behavioral analysis of masochism. *Journal of Experimental Research in Personality,* 1965, *1,* 65–70.

Brown, J. S., Martin, R. C. & Morrow, M. W. Self-punitive behavior in the rat: Facilitative effects of punishment on resistance to extinction. *Journal of Comparative and Physiological Psychology,* 1964, *57*(1), 127–133.

Bruning, J. Y., Copage, J. E., Kozuk, G. F., Young, P. & Young, W. E. Socially induced drive and range of cue utilization. *Journal of Personality and Social Psychology,* 1968, *9*(3), 242–244.

Butler, J. M. The interaction of client and therapist. *Journal of Abnormal Psychology,* 1952, *47,* 366–378.

Butler, J. M. & Rice, L. N. Adience, self-actualization, and drive theory. In J. M. Wepman and R. W. Heine (Eds.), *Concepts of personality.* Chicago: Aldine-Atherton, Inc., 1963. Pp. 79–110.

Cahoon, D. D. Symptom substitution and the behavior therapies: A reappraisal. *Psychological Bulletin,* March 1968, *69*(3), 149–156.

Cameron, N. *Personality development and psychotherapy: A dynamic approach.* Boston: Houghton Mifflin, 1963.

Carkhuff, R. R. *Helping and human relationships.* New York: Holt, Rinehart and Winston, 1969.

Carkhuff, R. R. & Berenson, B. G. *Beyond counselling and therapy.* New York: Holt, Rinehart and Winston, 1967.

Carkhuff, R. R. & Pierce, R. Differential effects of therapist race and social class upon patient depth of self-exploration in the initial clinical interview. *Journal of Consulting Psychology,* 1967, *31,* 632–634.

145

Cartwright, D. S. Effectiveness of psychotherapy: A critique of the spontaneous remission argument. *Journal of Counseling Psychology*, 1955, *2*, 290–296.

Cattell, R. B. The nature and measurement of anxiety. *Scientific American*, 1963, *208*(3), 96–104.

Cautela, J. R. Behavior therapy and self-control: Techniques and implications. In C. M. Franks (Ed.), *Behavior therapy: Appraisal and status.* New York: McGraw-Hill, 1969. Pp. 323–340.

Cofer, C. N. & Appley, M. H. *Motivation: Theory and research.* New York: John Wiley & Sons, 1964.

Cooke, G. The efficacy of two desensitization procedures: An analogue study. *Behaviour Research and Therapy*, 1966, *4*, 17–24.

D'Alessio, G. R. The concurrent use of behavior modification and psychotherapy. *Psychotherapy Theory, Research, and Practice*, 1968, *5*, 154–159.

Davison, G. C. Systematic desensitization as a counterconditioning process. *Journal of Abnormal Psychology*, 1968, *73*, 91–99.

DeCharmes, R., Levy, J., & Wertheimer, M. A note on attempted evaluations of psychotherapy. *Journal of Clinical Psychology*, 1954, *10*, 233–235.

Dollard, J. & Miller, N. E. *Personality and psychotherapy: An analysis in terms of learning, thinking and culture.* New York: McGraw-Hill, 1950.

Dreyfus, E. A. Counseling and existentialism. *Journal of Counseling Psychology*, 1962, *9*, 123–132.

Easterbrook, J. A. The effect of emotion on cue utilization and the organization of behavior. *Psychological Review*, 1959, *66*(3).

Ellis, A. Requisite conditions for basic personality change. *Journal of Consulting Psychology*, 1959, *23*, 538–540.

Ellis, A. *Reason and emotion in psychotherapy.* New York: Lyle Stuart, 1962.

Emery, J. R. & Krumboltz, J. D. Standard versus individualized hierarchies in desensitization to reduce test anxiety. *Journal of Counseling Psychology*, 1967, *14*, 204–209.

Eriksen, C. W. & Kuethe, J. L. Avoidance conditioning of verbal behavior without awareness: A paradigm of repression. *Journal of Abnormal and Social Psychology*, 1956, *53*, 203–209.

Eysenck, H. J. The effects of psychotherapy: An evaluation. *Journal of Consulting Psychology*, 1952, *16*, 319–327.

Eysenck, H. J. A reply to Luborsky's note. *British Journal of Psychology*, 1954, *45*, 132–133.

Eysenck, H. J. The effects of psychotherapy: A reply. *Journal of Abnormal and Social Psychology*, 1955, *50*, 147–148. (a)

Eysenck, H. J. Review of C. R. Rogers and R. F. Dymond, Psychotherapy and personality change. *British Journal of Psychology*, 1955, *46*, 237–238. (b)

Eysenck, H. J. *Handbook of abnormal psychology.* New York: Basic Books, 1961.

Eysenck, H. J. The outcome problem in psychotherapy: A reply. *Psychotherapy*, 1964, *1*, 97–100.

Fagan, J. & Shepherd, I. L. (Eds.) *Gestalt therapy now.* Palo Alto, California: Science and Behavior Books, Inc., 1970.

146

Farber, I. E. Response fixation under anxiety and non-anxiety conditions. *Journal of Experimental Psychology,* April 1948, *38*(2), 111–131.

Fenichel, O. Problems of psychoanalytic technique. Albany, N. Y.: *Psychoanalytic Quarterly,* 1941.

Fiedler, F. E. Comparison of therapeutic relationships in psychoanalytic, nondirective and Adlerian therapy. *Journal of Consulting Psychology,* 1950, *14,* 436–445.

Fiedler, F. E. Factor analysis of psychoanalytic, non-directive and Adlerian therapeutic relationships. *Journal of Consulting Psychology,* 1951, *15,* 32–38.

Ford, D. H. & Urban, H. B. *Systems of psychotherapy: A comparative study.* New York: John Wiley & Sons, 1963.

Frank, J. D. *Persuasion and healing: A comparative study of psychotherapy.* Baltimore: The Johns Hopkins Press, 1961.

Franks, C. M. *Behavior therapy: Appraisal and status.* New York: McGraw-Hill, 1969.

Freud, S. *An outline of psychoanalysis.* Vol. 23. London: Hogarth Press, 1935.

Fromm-Reichmann, Frieda. *Principles of intensive psychotherapy.* Chicago: Phoenix Books, University of Chicago Press, 1950.

Glover, Edward. *An investigation of the technique of psychoanalysis.* Baltimore: Williams and Wilkins Company, 1940.

Goldstein, K. *Human nature in the light of psychopathology.* Cambridge: Harvard University Press, 1940.

Goodstein, L. D. Conditioning therapy. *Contemporary Psychology,* 1967, *12* (4), 188.

Grosz, R. D. Effect of client expectations on the counselling relationship. *Personnel and Guidance Journal,* 1968, *46,* 797–800.

Harper, R. A. *Psychoanalysis and psychotherapy.* Englewood Cliffs, N. J.: Prentice-Hall, 1959.

Harway, N. I., Dittmann, A. T., Raush, H. L., Bordin, E. S. & Rigler, D. The measurement of depth of interpretation. *Journal of Consulting Psychology,* 1953, *19,* 247–253.

Hastings, D. N. Follow-up results in psychiatric illness. *American Journal of Psychiatry,* 1958, *114,* 1057–1066.

Horney, Karen. *Our inner conflicts: A constructive theory of neurosis.* New York: W. W. Norton, 1945.

Hovland, C. I. & Sears, R. R. Experiments on motor conflicts and their modes of resolution. *Journal of Experimental Psychology,* 1938, *23,* 477–493.

Hunt, H. F. & Dyrud, J. E. Commentary: Perspective in behavior therapy. In J. M. Shlien (Ed.), *Research in psychotherapy,* Vol. 3. Washington: American Psychological Association, 1968. Pp. 140–152.

Janis, I. L., Mahl, G. F., Kagan, J. & Holt, R. R. *Personality: Dynamics, development and assessment.* New York: Harcourt, Brace & World, 1969.

Johnson, S. M. The effects of desensitization and relaxation in the treatment of test anxiety. Unpublished master's thesis, Northwestern University, 1966.

Jones, M. C. A laboratory study of fear: The case of Peter. *Journal of Genetic Psychology,* 1924, *31,* 308–315.

Jung, C. G. *Collected works*. H. Read, M. Fordham, & G. Adler, Eds. Princeton: Princeton University Press, 1953.

Katahn, M., Strenger, S. & Cherry, N. Group counseling and behavior therapy with test-anxious college students. *Journal of Consulting Psychology*, 1966, *30*(6), 544–549.

Kiesler, D. J. Some myths of psychotherapy research and the search for a paradigm. *Psychological Bulletin*, 1966, *65*(2), 110–136.

Kiesler, D. J. A grid model for theory and research in the psychotherapies. In L. D. Eron & R. Callahan (Eds.), *The relation of theory to practice in psychotherapy*. Chicago: Aldine Press, 1969. Pp. 115–145.

Klein, M. H., Dittmann, A. T., Parloff, M. B. & Gill, M. M. Behavior therapy: Observations and reflections. *Journal of Consulting and Clinical Psychology*, 1969, *33*(3), 259–266.

Kreitman, N. The reliability of psychiatric diagnosis. *Journal of Mental Science*, 1961, *107*, 876–886.

Lang, P. J. Behavior therapy with a case of nervous anorexia. In L. P. Ullman & L. Krasner (Eds.), *Case studies in behavior modification*. New York: Holt, Rinehart and Winston, 1965. Pp. 217–221.

Lang, P. J. & Lazovik, A. D. Experimental desensitization of a phobia. *Journal of Abnormal and Social Psychology*, 1963, *66*, 519–525.

Lazarus, A. A. Group therapy of phobic disorders by systematic desensitization. *Journal of Abnormal and Social Psychology*, 1961, *63*, 504–510.

Lazarus, A. A. In support of technical eclecticism. *Psychological Reports*, 1967, *21*, 415–416.

London, P. *The modes and morals of psychotherapy*. New York: Holt, Rinehart and Winston, 1964.

Luborsky, L. A note on Eysenck's article: "The effects of psychotherapy: An evaluation." *British Journal of Psychology*, 1954, *45*, 129–131.

Lundin, R. W. *Personality: A behavioral analysis*. London: The Macmillan Company-Collier-Macmillan Limited, 1969.

Maher, B. A. *Principles of psychopathology: An experimental approach*. New York: McGraw-Hill, 1966.

Marmor, J. (Ed.) *Modern psychoanalysis*. New York: Basic Books, 1968.

Martin, D. G. *Introduction to psychotherapy*. Monterey, California: Brooks/Cole, 1971.

Martin, R. C. & Moon, T. L. Self-punitive behavior and periodic punishment. *Psychonomic Science*, 1968, *10*(7), 245–246.

Maslow, A. H. Dynamics of personality organization. *Psychological Review*, 1943, L, 519–524.

Menaker, T. Anxiety about drinking in alcoholics. *Journal of Abnormal and Social Psychology*, 1967, *72*, 43–49.

Menninger, K. *Theory of psychoanalytic technique*. New York: Harper & Row, 1958.

Menninger, K. *The vital balance: The life process in mental health and illness*. New York: The Viking Press, 1963.

Miller, J. G. & Butler, J. M. Book reviews. *Psychological Bulletin*, 1952, *49*, 183–185.

Miller, N. E. Experimental studies of conflict. In J. McV. Hunt (Ed.), *Personality and the behavior disorders*. New York: Ronald Press, 1944. Pp. 431–465.

148

Miller, N. E. Studies of fear as an acquirable drive: I. Fear as motivation and fear-reduction as reinforcement in the learning of new responses. *Journal of Experimental Psychology*, 1948, *38*, 89–101.

Miller, N. E. Comments on theoretical models illustrated by the development of a theory of conflict behavior. *Journal of Personality*, 1951, *20*, 82–100.

Miller, N. E. Liberalization of basic S-R concepts: Extensions to conflict behavior, motivation, and social learning. *Psychology: A study of a science.* New York: McGraw-Hill, 1959. Pp. 196–292.

Miller, N. E. & Kraeling, D. Displacement: Greater generalization of approach than avoidance in a generalized approach-avoidance conflict. *Journal of Experimental Psychology*, 1952, *43*, 217–221.

Miller, N. E. & Murray, E. J. Displacement and conflict: Learnable drive as a basis for the steeper gradient of avoidance than of approach. *Journal of Experimental Psychology*, 1952, *43*, 227–231.

Naar, R. Client-centered and behavior therapies: Their peaceful co-existence: A case study. *Journal of Abnormal Psychology*, 1970, *76*(1), 155–160.

Ornston, P. S., Cicchetti, D. V., Levine, J. & Fierman, L. B. Some parameters of verbal behavior that reliably differentiate novice from experienced psychotherapists. *Journal of Abnormal Psychology*, 1968, *73*, 240–244.

Parsons, L. B. & Parker, G. V. C. Personal attitudes, clinical appraisals, and verbal behavior of trained and untrained therapists. *Journal of Consulting and Clinical Psychology*, 1968, *32*, 64–71.

Patterson, C. H. *Theories of counseling and psychotherapy.* New York: Harper & Row, 1966.

Paul, G. L. *Insight vs. desensitization in psychotherapy: An experiment in anxiety reduction.* Stanford, Calif.: Stanford University Press, 1966.

Paul, G. L. Insight versus desensitization in psychotherapy two years after termination. *Journal of Consulting Psychology*, 1967, *31*, 333–348.

Paul, G. L. Two-year follow-up of systematic desensitization of therapy groups. *Journal of Abnormal Psychology*, 1968, *73*, 119–130.

Paul, G. L. Outcome of systematic desensitization. I: Background procedures, and uncontrolled reports of individual treatment. In C. M. Franks (Ed.), *Behavior therapy: Appraisal and status.* New York: McGraw-Hill, 1969. Pp. 63–105.

Paul, G. L. & Shannon, D. T. Treatment of anxiety through systematic desensitization in therapy groups. *Journal of Abnormal Psychology*, 1966, *71*, 124–135.

Pavlov, I. P. *Conditioned reflexes and psychiatry.* New York: International Publishers, 1941.

Perls, F., Hefferline, R. F. & Goodman, P. *Gestalt therapy.* New York: Dell Publishing, 1951.

Phillips, E. L. *Psychotherapy: A modern theory and practice.* Englewood Cliffs, N. J.: Prentice-Hall, 1956.

Phillips, E. L. & Johnston, M. H. S. Theoretical and clinical aspects of short term, parent-child psychotherapy. *Psychiatry*, 1954, *7*, 267–275.

Pierce, R. M. & Drasgow, J. Nondirective reflection vs conflict attention:

An empirical evaluation. *Journal of Clinical Psychology*, 1969, *25*, 341–342.

Rachman, S. Studies in desensitization, I: The separate effects of relaxation and desensitization. *Behaviour Research and Therapy*, 1965, *3*, 245–252.

Rachman, S. Studies in desensitization, II: Flooding. *Behaviour Research and Therapy*, 1966, *4*, 1–6. (a)

Rachman, S. Studies in desensitization, III: Speed of generalization. *Behaviour Research and Therapy*, 1966, *4*, 7–15. (b)

Raimy, V. C. Clinical methods: Psychotherapy. In C. P. Stone and D. W. Taylor (Eds.), *Annual review of psychology*. Vol. 3. Stanford, California: Annual Reviews, Inc., 1952. Pp. 321–350.

Rehm, L. P. & Marston, A. R. Reduction of social anxiety through modification of self-reinforcement: An instigation therapy technique. *Journal of Consulting and Clinical Psychology*, 1968, *32*(5), 565–574.

Reich, W. *Character analysis*. New York: Noonday Press, 1949.

Reik, T. *Listening with the third ear*. New York: Pyramid Publications, 1948.

Rice, L. N. Therapist's style of participation and case outcome. *Journal of Consulting Psychology*, 1965, *29*(2), 155–160.

Rice, L. N. & Wagstaff, A. K. Client voice quality and expressive style as indexes of productive psychotherapy. *Journal of Consulting Psychology*, 1967, *31*(6), 557–563.

Rogers, C. R. *Counseling and psychotherapy*. Boston: Houghton Mifflin, 1942.

Rogers, C. R. *Client-centered therapy*. Boston: Houghton Mifflin, 1951.

Rogers, C. R. The necessary and sufficient conditions of therapeutic personality change. *Journal of Consulting Psychology*, 1957, *21*, 95–103.

Rogers, C. R. A theory of therapy, personality, and interpersonal relationships, as developed in the client-centered framework. In S. Koch (Ed.), *Psychology: A study of a science*. Vol. 3. New York: McGraw-Hill, 1959. Pp. 184–256.

Rogers, C. R. *On becoming a person*. Boston: Houghton Mifflin, 1961.

Rogers, C. R. The interpersonal relationship: The core of guidance. *Harvard Educational Review*, 1962, *32*, 416–429.

Rogers, C. R. Psychotherapy today or where do we go from here? *American Journal of Psychotherapy*, 1963, *17*, 5–16.

Rogers, C. R. & Dymond, Rosalind F. *Psychotherapy and personality change*. Chicago: University of Chicago Press, 1954.

Rogers, C. R., Gendlin, E. T., Kiesler, D. J. & Truax, C. B. *The therapeutic relationship and its impact: A study of psychotherapy with schizophrenics*. Madison: The University of Wisconsin Press, 1967.

Rosenzweig, S. A reevaluation of psychotherapy: A reply to Hans Eysenck. *Journal of Abnormal and Social Psychology*, 1954, *49*, 298–304.

Rotter, J. B. *Social learning and clinical psychology*. Englewood Cliffs, N. J.: Prentice-Hall, 1954.

Rotter, J. B. Review of Joseph Wolpe, *Psychotherapy by reciprocal inhibition*. *Contemporary Psychology*, 1959, *4*(6), 176–178.

Sandifer, M. G., Jr., Pettus, C. & Quade, D. A study of psychiatric diagnosis. *Journal of Nervous and Mental Disease*, 1964, *139*, 350–356.

150

Saslow, G. & Peters, A. D. A follow-up study of "untreated" patients with various behavior disorders. *Psychiatric Quarterly,* 1956, *30,* 283–302.

Schofield, W. *Psychotherapy: The purchase of friendship.* Englewood Cliffs, N.J.: Prentice-Hall, 1964.

Shaffer, L. F. & Shoben, E. J. *The psychology of adjustment.* Boston: Houghton Mifflin, 1956.

Shannon, D. T. & Wolff, M. E. *The effects of modelling in reduction of snake phobia by systematic desensitization.* Urbana, Ill.: University of Illinois, 1967.

Shlien, J. M., Mosak, H. H., & Dreikurs, R. Effect of time limits: A comparison of two psychotherapies. *Journal of Counseling Psychology,* 1962, *9,* 31–34.

Shoben, E. J., Jr. Psychotherapy as a problem in learning theory. *Psychological Bulletin,* 1949, *46,* 366–392, 533.

Siegel, P. S. Motivation: Second act. *Contemporary Psychology,* 1965, *10*(3), 97–99.

Smith, M. B. "Mental health" reconsidered: A special case of the problem of values in psychology. *American Psychologist,* 1961, *16,* 299–306.

Speisman, J. C. Depth of interpretation and verbal resistance in psychotherapy. *Journal of Consulting Psychology,* 1959, *23,* 93–99.

Stevenson, I. The challenge of results in psychotherapy. *American Journal of Psychiatry,* 1959, *116,* 120–123.

Stevenson, I. Discussion of chapter 1. In J. Wolpe, A. Salter, & L. J. Reyna (Eds.), *The conditioning therapies.* New York: Holt, Rinehart and Winston, 1964. Pp. 17–20.

Stone, L. J. & Hokanson, J. E. Arousal reduction via self-punitive behavior. *Journal of Personality and Social Psychology,* 1969, *12*(1), 72–79.

Strupp, H. H. An objective comparison of Rogerian and psychoanalytic techniques. *Journal of Consulting Psychology,* 1955, *19,* 1–7. (a)

Strupp, H. H. Psychotherapeutic technique, professional affiliation, and experience level. *Journal of Consulting Psychology,* 1955, *19,* 97–102. (b)

Strupp, H. H. A multidimensional comparison of therapist activity in analytic and client-centered therapy. *Journal of Consulting Psychology,* 1957, *21,* 301–308.

Strupp, H. H. Nature of psychotherapist's contribution to treatment process. *Archives of General Psychiatry,* 1960, *3,* 219–231.

Strupp, H. H. The outcome problem in psychotherapy revisited. *Psychotherapy,* 1963, *1,* 1–13.

Strupp, H. H. & Bergin, A. E. Some empirical and conceptual bases for coordinated research in psychotherapy. *International Journal of Psychiatry,* 1969, *7*(2), 18–90.

Szasz, T. S. *The myth of mental illness.* New York: Holber, 1961.

Thorne, F. C. A critique of non-directive methods of psychotherapy. *Journal of Abnormal Psychology,* 1944, *39,* 459–470.

Thorne, F. C. Critique of recent developments in personality counseling theory. *Journal of Clinical Psychology,* 1957, *13,* 234–244.

Tomlinson, T. M. & Hart, J. T. A validation study of the process scale. *Journal of Consulting Psychology,* 1962, *26,* 74–78.

Truax, C. B. Reinforcement and non-reinforcement in Rogerian psychotherapy. *Journal of Abnormal and Social Psychology,* 1966, *71,* 1–9.

Truax, C. B. Effects of client-centered psychotherapy with schizophrenic patients: Nine years pretherapy and nine years post-therapy hospitalization. *Journal of Consulting and Clinical Psychology*, 1970, *35*, 417–422.

Truax, C. B. & Carkhuff, R. R. For better or for worse: The process of psychotherapeutic personality change. *Recent advances in the study of behaviour change*. Montreal: McGill University Press, 1963.

Truax, C. B. & Carkhuff, R. R. *Toward effective counseling and psychotherapy: Training and practice*. Chicago: Aldine, 1967.

Van Der Veen, F. Basic elements in the process of psychotherapy: A research study. *Journal of Consulting Psychology*, 1967, *31*(3), 295–303.

Volsky, T., Magoon, T. M., Norman, W. I. & Hoyt, D. P. *The outcome of counseling and psychotherapy: Theory and research*. Minneapolis: University of Minnesota Press, 1965.

Ward, C. H. Psychotherapy research: Dilemmas and directions. *Archives of General Psychiatry*, June 1964, *10*, 596–622. (Copyright 1964 by American Medical Association.)

Weitzman, B. Behavior therapy and psychotherapy. *Psychological Review*, 1967, *74*(4), 300–317.

Wolberg, L. R. *The technique of psychotherapy: 2nd edition*. New York: Grune and Stratton, 1967.

Wolpe, J. *Psychotherapy by reciprocal inhibition*. Stanford, California: Stanford University Press, 1958.

Wolpe, J. Presidential message. *Newsletter of the Association for Advancement of Behavior Therapy*, 1968, *3*, 1–2.

Worell, L. Some ramifications of exposure to conflict. In B. A. Maher (Ed.), *Progress in experimental personality research*. New York: Academic Press, 1967. Pp. 91–125.

Yates, A. J. *Frustration and conflict*. New York: John Wiley & Sons, 1962.

Zaffy, D. J. & Bruning, J. L. Drive and the range of cue utilization. *Journal of Experimental Psychology*, 1966, *71*(3), 382–384.

Index

Date Due

JAN 2 n 1997			
OCT 2 1 1997			
AP 2 9 '98			
SEP 1 7 2001			
NOV 1 0 2002			
JAN 2 6 2003			

PRINTED IN U.S.A.   CAT. NO. 24 161   BRO DART